Victor gave me a clear understanding of how to structure a case interview using a highly logical approach. This helped me get offers from BCG and a boutique firm and make it to McKinsey's final round before opting out. Thanks, Victor!

— Martin Pustilnick
Associate
Boston Consulting Group, Argentina

In my first attempt to break into consulting, I failed every one of my interviews with McKinsey, Bain, BCG, Oliver Wyman, Monitor, Booz and probably a few others. On my second attempt two years later, I followed everything Victor Cheng suggested and took advantage of every resource he provided...and received an offer from McKinsey!

— Daniel Suo
Business Analyst (Offer Recipient)
McKinsey, Stamford

Without Victor's help, I never would have gotten an offer from BCG. What he teaches really makes the difference between getting an offer and not.

— Puttipath Tasnavites
Associate
Boston Consulting Group, Thailand

After following Victor's guidance, I had a complete breakthrough in my case interview performance and got an offer from Monitor.

— Marine Serres
Senior Consultant
Monitor & Company

Coming from a non-top-tier business school, I received an offer from BCG by following Victor's advice.

— Andrew Chau
Associate
Boston Consulting Group, Canada
(On Leave to Consult for the United Nations)

As a PhD candidate in engineering, I had an academic background that left me completely unprepared for the case interview process. When I started, I looked at all the case preparation materials I could get my hands on. But none of these materials taught you how to think.

That's when I found Victor Cheng. Instead of asking you to memorize 12 different case systems or what question to ask exactly when, he teaches you how to think like a consultant.

After my case interviews, I learned that I'd solved cases that the interviewers hadn't seen anyone solve before, and I usually did so with ample time to spare. I ended up getting my dream job. Thank you, Victor!

> —Zach Jacobson
> Associate
> **McKinsey, New York**

Rather than 'teach to the test,' Victor teaches you how to think like a consultant. It's an approach that required me to memorize nothing more than a few simple business ideas yet allowed me to perform well in the case interview regardless of the type of case I received. I could not have gotten my BCG offer without his help. Thank you, Victor!

> —Warren Cheng
> Associate
> **Boston Consulting Group, Hong Kong**

Victor and all his materials on the case interview are by far the best resources on the topic that exist. In asking my interviewers for feedback between rounds, all three times they told me my performance was really strong and they could not think of anything that needed improvement.

This kind of feedback helped keep my confidence high so that I continued to perform well. The combination of Victor's advice and hard work made all the difference for me.

> —Dmitry Papulin
> Business Analyst
> **McKinsey, Dubai**

Victor taught me how to prepare both technically and mentally, and this is what makes the difference between him and the competitors.

The feedback I received after my first few case interviews was that I seemed to know what I was doing, was confident and demonstrated a thinking process that was well-structured.

Without Victor's help I probably wouldn't have gotten the offer from BCG. Thank you, Victor Cheng!

—István Mag
Associate Offer Recipient
Boston Consulting Group, Hungary

Victor is effective because he focuses on behaviors and habits that make you successful and not just on frameworks. With his help, I received a McKinsey Summer Associate offer.

—Abhi Patangay
Kellogg School of Management

Victor tells you not only what to do in an interview but also why you should do it. Knowing the logic and reasoning behind what consulting companies were looking for made it much easier to demonstrate my consulting strengths and resulted in my securing a summer position at BCG.

—James Nauss
Summer Associate
Boston Consulting Group, Canada

CASE INTERVIEW SECRETS

A FORMER MCKINSEY INTERVIEWER
REVEALS HOW TO GET MULTIPLE
JOB OFFERS IN CONSULTING

VICTOR CHENG

Innovation Press
Seattle

This book and the information contained herein are for informative purposes only. The information in this book is distributed on an as-is basis, without warranty. The author makes no legal claims, express or implied, and the material is not meant to substitute legal or financial counsel.

The author, publisher, and/or copyright holder assume no responsibility for the loss or damage caused or allegedly caused, directly or indirectly, by the use of information contained in this book. The author and publisher specifically disclaim any liability incurred from the use or application of the contents of this book.

All rights reserved. No part of this book may be reproduced or transmitted in any form by any means, including electronic, mechanical, photocopy, recording, or otherwise, without the prior written permission of the publisher.

Throughout this book, trademarked names are referenced. Rather than using a trademark symbol with every occurrence of a trademarked name, we state that we are using the names in an editorial fashion only and to the benefit of the trademark owner, with no intention of infringement of the trademark.

Published by Innovation Press
93 S. Jackson St., #75551, Seattle, WA 98104

Printed in the United States of America

ISBN 978-0-9841835-2-4

For Julia and the girls

FREE BONUS ITEMS

The free companion items to this book, including video demonstrations, printable versions of handouts, and book updates, are available at:

www.caseinterview.com/bonus

Please access these additional resources now before you forget.

ACKNOWLEDGMENTS

VERY FEW PEOPLE succeed entirely on their own. I'm no exception. I want to thank my parents who put me in educational environments where my talents had the room and opportunity to shine.

I also want to thank two people who helped me get my multiple job offers in consulting. The first is Josie Welling, a Stanford Graduate School of Business alumna and former Oliver Wyman consultant who gave me my first practice case interview. I didn't know Josie at all. We didn't have any friends in common or anything. I more or less out of the blue asked her to help, and she was generous enough to oblige. I was never able to pay her back, so I started thinking about how I could pay it forward. If Josie was willing to help out an eager undergrad, the least I could do was the same. The result is www.caseinterview.com. And while I receive a lot of emails from around the world thanking me for creating the site, I have to in turn thank Josie for her inspiration.

I also want to thank Kevin Lo, a former Bain intern and consultant who is a friend of a friend. He was kind enough to spend an hour with me on the phone and introduce me to the concept of a framework, which up until that point I had never heard of before. The frameworks you see in this book are based largely on the ones he shared with me during that phone call. I still have my original notes.

CONTENTS

PART ONE

Overview

Chapter 1

INTRODUCTION

IF YOU'RE APPLYING to a top strategy management consulting firm, you'll soon discover an unusual obstacle in your way — the case interview. It's a unique interview format that firms such as McKinsey & Company, Bain & Company, Boston Consulting Group (BCG), Oliver Wyman, A.T. Kearney, Monitor & Company, and Roland Berger use.

Firms use the case interview to evaluate candidates with wide-ranging backgrounds, from newly minted undergraduates, MBAs, and PhDs to experienced hires. The recruiting process differs slightly depending on candidates' education level, but the case interview portion of the recruiting process is, in most situations, nearly identical for everyone, and the advice in this book applies to candidates at all levels.

Before I explain what this book covers and how to get the most out of it, I'd like to share my background with you to give you a sense of where my perspective on case interviews comes from.

How I Learned What I Know about Case Interviews

When applying to the top consulting firms years ago, I encountered the case interview for the first time — and totally bombed. An interview that was supposed to have lasted 40 minutes ended after only 3.5 minutes! My reaction at the time was, "What the heck just happened?" My first impulse was to blame whoever invented this torturous process called a *case interview*.

Having earned perfect scores on my math college entrance exams and having finished my undergraduate coursework at Stanford in three years, I wasn't mentally prepared to be dismissed so soon after the interview had begun.

I quickly realized that none of my schoolwork had taught me how to do well in a case interview. It was a new skill—and arguably a far more important one than anything taught in any of my classes. And here's why: Whether I did well in any one class didn't materially affect whether I could work in consulting. If I got perfect grades in all my classes (which I didn't) but couldn't demonstrate mastery of the case interview, I would most certainly be rejected.

As an aspiring consultant, I soon understood that the single most profitable skill I could learn while in school did *not* have to do with English, math, psychology, history, economics, or science. The most profitable skill I could learn would help me pass the damn job interview! And in the management consulting industry, that job interview is the case interview.

Fortunately, my first case interview was only a trial run. I'd found a former management consultant at the Stanford Graduate School of Business and begged her to give me a practice interview. She agreed, and I bombed.

After that humiliating first attempt, I decided to make passing the case interview my No. 1 area of study. There was no good reason to spend 250 hours every quarter studying academics that alone would not directly get me a job; I needed to put at least as much effort into learning the one skill that could get me hired.

The path I took to learn about case interviews was ridiculously time-consuming. Books like this one and websites like mine (www.caseinterview.com) didn't exist back then.

I basically "infiltrated" this seemingly elite industry to beg people on the inside to share with me hints about how the case interview works. Hundreds of hours later, I had learned enough to assemble an overall picture of how the case interview process unfolds. I remember thinking at the time that it shouldn't have to be *this* hard just to learn how to do well in an interview.

A year after I spent more than 100 hours learning about case interviews, including participating in 50 practice interviews with friends, I interviewed with every consulting firm I applied to, including McKinsey, Bain, BCG, Booz, Oliver Wyman (formerly

Mercer Management Consulting), LEK, Monitor, and A.T. Kearney.

I received a total of six consulting job offers, from McKinsey, Bain, Oliver Wyman, LEK, Monitor, and A.T. Kearney. (I voluntarily dropped out of my Booz final round, and I did not pass my first-round interview at BCG.)

After passing 60 case interviews out of 61 attempts, I accepted an offer from McKinsey. Of the 400 Stanford students who had applied for jobs with McKinsey, only six received job offers—a 1.5 percent acceptance rate. Had I known this statistic before I applied, I would have been far too intimidated even to try.

Success as a job seeker is not the only factor that has shaped my perspective of the case interview; my experience working in consulting has too. At McKinsey, I was one of the firm's rising stars and even conducted case interviews (in addition to reading applicants' cover letters and résumés). About 100 people were in my starting class when I joined McKinsey as a business analyst. Two years later, only ten 10 of us globally were promoted directly to associate (the post-MBA, post-PhD position). The remaining 90 were asked to leave the firm permanently or attend business school, or were directed to continue their work as business analysts. I was in that elite group of consultants in the top 10 percent *globally*—and at 24 years old was one of the youngest associates in McKinsey history.

Through this promotion I learned how consulting firms work and how consultants think. I also learned *why* consultants, who also serve as case interviewers, ask the questions they do in the interview process. An interviewee who understands life on the job can better anticipate what these firms are looking for in candidates. I will share this knowledge with you throughout the pages that follow.

During my time at McKinsey, I read cover letters and résumés from applicants and also conducted case interviews.

Thus, my perspective on case interviews is based on my experience as (1) a multiple-job-offer candidate, (2) a top 10 percent McKinsey consultant, and (3) a case interviewer. In short, I've developed an uncommon insight into the case interview from having been on both sides of the table, and that's what I share with you here.

How This Book Is Organized

I've organized this book into seven parts.

Part One provides a big-picture view of the case interview process and the different types of evaluation tools used.

Part Two covers quantitative assessments. Though not technically case interviews, quantitative assessments are often injected into the recruiting process before or during hypothetical-situation, or "real," case interviews.

Part Three addresses the fundamentals of tackling "real" case interviews. You'll discover the core problem-solving tools needed to succeed in any case interview.

Part Four discusses the primary frameworks you'll use to solve the business problems presented in the case interview.

Part Five covers the traditional candidate-led case interview format, which is the oldest and most common approach. New case interview variations have emerged over the past few years, but they all are derived in large part from the original candidate-led format. This section offers plenty of suggestions, by way of numerous examples and practice tips, for honing your case interview skills.

Part Six describes the other types of case formats and how to handle them successfully. It also provides useful tips for practicing and mastering your case interview skills.

Part Seven discusses how to pull all the skills together to get the job offer.

How to Get the Interview

This book focuses on how to pass the case interview. Of course, to pass the interview, it helps to get the interview first! For more information on getting the interview, I recommend that you read my free online tutorials on this subject:

- www.caseinterview.com/jump/resume
- www.caseinterview.com/jump/cover-letter

How to Stay Current on Case Interview Developments

Consulting firms are under enormous pressure to compete for the best talent—to find the hidden gems in a quarry of rocks. As part of that ongoing effort, the firms continually evolve their recruiting methods.

To keep you current on the latest case interview developments, I publish an email newsletter with the latest insights on what the major consulting firms are doing *right now*.

With tens of thousands of visitors a month to my website and a global network of aspiring consultants in 100 countries, I receive *daily* emails from around the world keeping me up to date. In turn, I keep my newsletter readers up to date.

My readers knew about the opening of McKinsey's new Nigeria office even before the news appeared on McKinsey's website. One day after BCG started experimenting with a problem-solving test in Scandinavia, my readers were learning how to prepare for it. When Bain Western Europe started testing a written case interview, my readers found out by the end of that same week and were given tips on how to prepare for it.

In addition, my website includes video demonstrations of many of the techniques described in this book, as well as printable versions of many of the key diagrams that appear in these pages. To receive my real-time updates, the video demonstrations, and the printable diagrams, visit www.caseinterview.com/bonus.

I recommend visiting the website right now, while it's fresh in your mind, to guarantee that you do not miss out on these important, free companion resources.

Chapter 2

THE SEVEN TYPES OF EVALUATION TOOLS

STRATEGY CONSULTING FIRMS use the term *case interview* to describe several methods of assessing a candidate's problem-solving abilities. Firms have been modifying the traditional case interview format to add their own twists, thereby creating many different types of case interviews. Today, the major consulting firms use seven primary formats grouped into two categories: (1) quantitative assessments, and (2) hypothetical-situation case interviews.

Even though quantitative assessments are not technically case interviews, I've included them here for two reasons. First, many of the written quantitative assessments include a mini case as part of the assessment process. Second, sometimes interviewers give candidates a quantitative assessment in the middle of a hypothetical-situation case interview. Because consulting firms intertwine these two categories of evaluation tools, you will need to familiarize yourself with both.

Below are overviews of the various case interview formats. I address how to tackle each type of case in subsequent chapters. The following summaries will give you some idea of what interviewers expect from you.

Quantitative Assessments

Format #1: The Quantitative Test

The quantitative test assesses math skills, data interpretation, and numerical critical-reasoning skills. For example, a math skills question would evaluate your ability to do arithmetic, fractions, and percentage calculations. A data interpretation question would ask you to examine a chart or graph and determine which of four conclusions would *not* be supported by the chart. A numerical critical-reasoning question would use words and numerical data to test your reasoning abilities: "Assuming the data in chart A is true, sales of product A increase by 10 percent, and sales of product B decline by 15 percent, should the client proceed with the proposed decision?"

Among the major firms, McKinsey was first to incorporate this type of assessment into its recruiting process. McKinsey named its version the McKinsey Problem Solving Test (also known as the McKinsey PST), which is discussed in more detail in Chapter 3. For additional information on the McKinsey PST, including sample questions and sample tests, visit www.caseinterview.com/jump/pst.

Because quantitative assessments such as the McKinsey PST involve many computations during a timed exam, you'll need to practice your basic arithmetic for both speed *and* accuracy. To facilitate the improvement of these skills among my readers, I've developed a case interview math drill. This tool gives you practice math questions on a timed practice exam and allows you to compare your performance to that of other candidates, so you'll know if you're faster at math than 25 percent, 50 percent, or 75 percent of other users. You can access this free tool here: www.caseinterviewmath.com.

Format #2: The Estimation Question

The estimation question tests a candidate's ability to do math and use assumptions to simplify complicated math problems so they can be solved with only pen and paper.

An estimation question involves the interviewer asking you to estimate some number without the benefit of any research or access to Google. Typically, you'll be asked to estimate the size of a particular market. Below are a few examples of estimation questions:

- How many gallons (or liters) of gasoline does a typical filling station pump each week?

- Assume the year is 1980, and Motorola just invented a new technology called the cellular phone. The first three years of revenues for this technology have been terrible.

As manufacturing costs and prices decline, what will sales for cellular phones be in 1985? Justify your estimate.

- How long does it take to relocate an average-size mountain 10 miles elsewhere using an average-size dump truck?

You might be wondering if these odd questions represent *actual* interview questions. Well, interviewers asked me these questions during my own interview process, so I can assure you that they very much represent the type of questions you may be asked.

Remember: The only tools you will be given are a pen and a piece of paper. There's no web access, Google, or calculator. And to make things even more challenging, the interviewer expects an answer in five to seven minutes.

It's impossible to determine the answer to these questions *accurately*, given the constraints, but one can *estimate* an answer by (1) making a few simplifying assumptions, and (2) doing math. Interviewers ask these questions more to assess *how* you answer them and less to assess the accuracy of your answer.

You're probably thinking this must be the way consulting firms torture candidates, because that was my initial reaction. But once I started working at McKinsey, I realized that *clients* ask consultants these questions all the time. So if you want to blame someone for what you endure in the recruiting process, blame the clients. It's their fault.

Hypothetical-Situation Case Interview

Format #3: The Candidate-Led Case Interview

In the traditional candidate-led case interview, the interviewer (the person pretending to be the client) asks you an incredibly ambiguous question such as "Should we enter the Latin American market?" or "We're losing a lot of money, so how do we fix it?"

After the interviewer asks you the opening question, he will promptly stop talking—for the rest of the interview. You can ask the interviewer questions and request certain types of data, and some interviewers will give you hints, but others will sit silently for 30 minutes unless you request specific pieces of data.

Because of the enormous ambiguity of this type of case and the lack of direction from the interviewer, we call this a *candidate-led case interview*. Because this format is the foundation upon which the other types of case interview formats are built, I've devoted an entire section of this book to how to solve this type of case.

Format #4: The Interviewer-Led Case Interview

Although the interviewer-led case interview requires the same problem-solving skills as the candidate-led case interview, the dynamic between interviewer and candidate differs significantly in each instance. McKinsey uses the interviewer-led format nearly exclusively, so you will want to familiarize yourself with how this format is applied. Its two distinguishing features are as follows:

1. The *interviewer* (not you) determines which parts of the case are important, decides which questions are worth asking, asks you those questions, and then expects you to answer them. In contrast, in the candidate-led interview, *you* decide which questions are worth asking to solve the client's problem, and *you* find the answers to your own questions.

2. The flow of the case is very *abrupt*. If a case has four key areas, in a traditional case you would determine which of the four areas is most important, analyze the first area, move on to the second most important area, determine your conclusion, and present that conclusion. In the interviewer-led case, the interviewer might ask you which of the four areas you think is most important and why and then (regardless of how you answer) say, "Let's tackle area number four." (This can happen even if you thought that area was least important.) In an interviewer-led case, you *jump around a lot*, which can be unsettling if you don't anticipate it happening.

Format #5: The Written Case Interview

In a written case interview, you are given a lot of charts and exhibits; expect somewhere between 5 and 40. Typically you'll be given an hour or two to review all the information, and then you'll be asked to take a written test about the case.

Other variations include starting a case in written format and finishing it in another format, such as a group or presentation-only case interview.

Format #6: The Group Case Interview

In a group case interview, the interviewer presents a case problem to you and, typically, three other candidates. The interviewer gives you and your teammates several exhibits, poses an open-ended question, and expects you to work with each other to solve the case. (Hint: You do well in this case by helping your "competitors"—the other candidates—do well, not by shooting them down.)

Format #7: The Presentation-Only Case Interview

The presentation-only case overlaps partially with the written case. As in the written case interview, you will typically be presented with a large stack of charts and exhibits, given an hour or two to analyze the information, and then be expected to create a slide presentation of your findings and recommendations. After preparing your presentation, you meet the interviewer for the first time. Your presentation is the sole factor the interviewer uses to decide whether you pass the case. The interviewer never observes your analysis or problem-solving skills—only how you present the results of your analysis and problem solving.

The next section covers how to handle quantitative assessments, and the rest of the book describes how to handle hypothetical-situation, or "real," case interviews. I'll start by introducing you to some foundational concepts and tools and then tackle the various case interview formats. Let's get started with quantitative assessments.

PART TWO

Quantitative
Assessments

Chapter 3

MCKINSEY PROBLEM SOLVING TEST

MANY FIRMS USE problem-solving tests to evaluate a candidate's math, logic, and analytical skills. Of the major firms, McKinsey headed in this direction first, and Bain and BCG have experimented with this approach in some countries. Because other firms' tests are similar to McKinsey's, I will use the McKinsey Problem Solving Test as our primary example.

The McKinsey PST does *not* require that you be business savvy in order to perform well. It is primarily a math, estimation, logic, and critical-thinking test written to be accessible to people with nonbusiness backgrounds and from a variety of countries and cultures. In some respects, having some business background could be a bit of a liability in this situation. Someone with an analytical and logical bent will take the questions and data literally — which is good.

I suggest you *read each question carefully*. If you rush, you might think a question is familiar and quickly answer the question you *think* is being asked. Instead, answer the *literal* question being asked, using the *actual* data presented.

How to Prepare

In preparing for the McKinsey PST, consider the following suggestions:

- Take sample tests from McKinsey and some of the other firms that use a similar process. The upside is that these are the most realistic representations of the real tests. The downside is that there are very few sample tests available online, so you likely will go through them quickly.

- Practice some of the fundamental skills that the McKinsey PST evaluates. One of the main skills evaluated is how to solve a math word problem — a verbal description of a situation for which you have to figure out the type of math computation required, given what is asked. This general skill is very useful on the job as a consultant.

Another fundamental skill is data interpretation—you have data in charts, graphs, and tables, but what does it mean? Which data is necessary to answer the question? Which data is just a distraction?

Math and numerical critical-reasoning skills are like muscles—the more you use them, the stronger you get. To sharpen these skills, I recommend using a subset of questions from GRE practice tests. If you become extremely proficient and efficient in answering the straightforward math questions that are, relatively speaking, easier to prepare for in advance, you maximize the time you have available during the test to answer the more complicated, multipart questions that require math computation, data sufficiency, and critical-reasoning skills.

Note that the math, numerical critical-reasoning, and data interpretation practice resources help with only 50 to 70 percent of the test. They do not cover the whole McKinsey PST.

- Practice the speed and accuracy of your arithmetic. The McKinsey PST is a timed test designed to identify only those who are very good at math and logical thinking. Even if you are really good at math, you will *barely* finish the test. Even if you have a PhD in physics or math, it is *very important* that you practice your math computations. I have received many emails from engineers who had 4.0 GPAs in school yet did not pass the PST. Flex those math skills often and they'll only get stronger.

Practice Resources

Because these tests evolve over time, I have a resource guide on my website with up-to-date links to practice resources, sample questions, and sample tests: www.caseinterview.com/jump/pst. I also provide a tool to help with arithmetic speed and accuracy: www.caseinterviewmath.com.

This is a tool I developed for practicing (1) arithmetic for speed and accuracy (both *very* important on the McKinsey PST), and (2) estimation math with large numbers (useful for solving some of the McKinsey PST word problems faster, when precise math isn't necessary to answer the question and just an estimate will suffice). This tool compares your math accuracy and speed to those of other www.caseinterview.com members and to my own test results to give you an idea of how your math skills compare to your peers'.

Chapter 4

ESTIMATION QUESTIONS

CONSULTING FIRMS ASK estimation questions during interviews for several practical reasons. In consulting, clients often ask you to evaluate dozens of potential opportunities. A single engagement easily can cost a client $1 million to $3 million, so the cost of carefully analyzing each opportunity in excruciating detail can get quite expensive quickly.

Often consultants determine whether an opportunity is worth considering by evaluating whether the estimated financial impact is even *remotely close* to the minimum financial return expected. Using this estimation skill can easily eliminate 80 percent of the opportunities from consideration.

For example, I recently worked with a client to develop options to grow the business. The executive team came up with 30 different possibilities, but the company, being relatively small, simply did not have the manpower to analyze, let alone pursue, 30 new revenue streams simultaneously.

Using a marker and flip chart, I worked with the client to estimate the best-case-scenario revenue impact for each opportunity. I asked the client the following questions: What percentage of the existing customer base would be prospective buyers of the new product? In the best-case scenario, what percentage would realistically buy? What is the maximum price you could realistically charge? Once the client answered these questions, I said, "If we put all those (micro-)estimates together, I get a best-case-scenario estimate of $X million in revenue, assuming everything goes absolutely perfectly."

The executive team members had been debating for years about whether to invest in this new product, but nobody had actually done an estimation analysis. When the team members saw the best-case-scenario figure, they unanimously decided it wasn't worth the headache for such little revenue. We killed the idea on the spot and ended a three-year debate in just ten minutes.

Clients value the ability to resolve long-standing debates of *opinions*, using *estimates* based on reasonable *assumptions*. And if clients value something, then consulting firm partners value finding people who can give clients what they want. Given this context, you can see why interviewers ask estimation questions.

Computation-Level Estimates

To effectively answer estimation questions based on a set of basic facts that provide a snapshot of a particular situation, you must be able to (1) do mental math with larger numbers, and (2) round numbers intelligently.

Estimation Skill #1: Doing Precise Arithmetic with Large Numbers

Let's begin with a sample question: If we have a market of 2 million buyers and assume a market share of 15 percent and an average revenue per buyer of $300, what's the estimated revenue impact for this opportunity?

Ideally, you need to be able to do these computations in your head or, at most, with only a pen and a piece of paper. Doing math with large numbers isn't about being a human calculator, though many people disagree with me about that. The trick is to *simplify* the problem before you attempt to solve it. Let me illustrate using the example above. If we draw out the equation in the order it is given, it appears as follows:

$$\text{Revenue} = 2 \text{ million buyers} \times 15\% \text{ market share} \times \$300$$
$$\text{revenue per buyer}$$

Most people gravitate to solving a math problem in exactly the form in which it is presented, but it's often easier to simplify the problem into a series of smaller problems. For example, I notice that the first number ($2 million) and the last number ($300) are easy numbers to multiply, so I would mentally rewrite the equation as follows:

$$(2 \text{ million} \times \$300) \times 15\%$$

That works out to:

$$\$600 \text{ million} \times 15\%$$

Now I notice there is a percentage. I don't like dealing with percentages, because it means I need to change a decimal point. I'm wary of decimal point changes (seriously!), because when you're dealing with a lot of zeros, it's very easy to misplace a decimal. So I try to move decimal points only when the math is very simple. When the math is complex *and* I need to move decimal points, it's too easy for me to screw up.

Looking at the following equation, I think about which type of operation (multiplication or division) will be less confusing to tackle. I go with multiplication. The formula is currently:

$$\$600 \text{ million} \times 15\%$$

In my head, I visualize it as:

$$(\$600 \text{ million} \times 10\%) + (\$600 \text{ million} \times 5\%)$$

I also note that the second half of the formula, ($600 million x 5%), is exactly half of the first part, ($600 million x 10%). All I need to do is solve the first part of the formula and split it in half in order to get the second half:

$$\$600 \text{ million} \times 10\% = \$60 \text{ million}$$

$$1/2 \times \$60 \text{ million} = \$30 \text{ million}$$

$$\$60 \text{ million} + \$30 \text{ million} = \$90 \text{ million}$$

This seems like a lot of steps to go through, but the point is that you can quickly simplify the problem so you can solve it easily in your head. Often it is much easier to solve a long series of simple math problems than a short series of complicated ones. You may not need to break down this problem into as many simpler parts as I did, but the process of doing so is important when it comes to passing quantitative assessment tests.

In the example above, I simplified the problem enough that I felt comfortable doing the math computations in my head. You can simplify a problem in any mathematically correct way you choose. The secret here is to become accustomed to rearranging a large-numbers math problem into a simpler format *before* you compute anything.

As with any new habit or skill, you will want to practice this math-simplification skill. You can do so by using the large-numbers math practice tool available here: www.caseinterviewmath.com.

Your initial attempts will be somewhat slow, but you'll pick up speed as you become accustomed to the process. With sufficient practice, you'll be able to solve increasingly complicated math problems without using a calculator.

Estimation Skill #2: Rounding Numbers Intelligently

The previous demonstration illustrated how to simplify a complex math problem into a series of smaller ones, which is useful when you need an "exact" answer. In many situations, however, you don't need such a precise answer.

My clients who were analyzing potential revenue opportunities didn't care if a product could generate $1.1 million in sales versus $1.2 million in sales, because the minimum cutoff for a new product launch was $10 million. The numbers were so far from the cutoff that the opportunities didn't matter. This type of situation requires a "directionally correct" answer as opposed to a "precise" one.

The first step in intelligently rounding numbers is to recognize *when* you're looking for a directionally correct answer only and therefore can round numbers. Once you know you can round, you'll want to round numbers in an intelligent way.

For example, let's say we have another estimation computation to tackle, this time for a market with 54 million buyers, 17.5 percent market share, and average revenue per customer of $300. We need a directionally correct answer only.

At first glance, I realize there's no way I can do this math in my head without making a mistake. But then I remember I don't need an exact answer ... only a directionally correct one. It's time to round numbers, and here's how I do it. Pay attention not only to the math but also to my thought process and rationale for why I make certain adjustments. I start with the following formula:

$$54 \text{ million} \times 17.5\% \times \$300$$

I look at 54 million and say to myself, "OK, that's too hard a number to work with. I need to get it to a round number. I could round down to 50 million or up to 60 million. Geez, 50 million seems easier to work with, and it's only a 4 million difference instead of 6 million. OK, I'm rounding to 50 million." So now I am seeing in my head (or perhaps on paper):

$$50 \text{ million} \times 17.5\% \times \$300$$

In addition, because I rounded 54 million *down* to 50 million, I need to remember that my current estimate is going to be too *low*. So I don't have to occupy mental space trying to remember this, I point my finger down toward the ground as a physical reminder that my estimate is too low.

It is very important to keep track of whether your estimate will be too high or too low. You don't need to keep track of how much you'll be off by; you just need to know if your estimate will be too high or too low.

Back to the computation, we now have:

50 million x 17.5% x $300 (+ a finger pointing to the floor)

The next figure I don't like is 17.5 percent. I have a decimal in there, and 17 is a hard number to work with. Well, I could round to 15 percent or to 20 percent, and both are 2.5 percent off the actual number. But 20 percent is easier to work with, so if I can find another good reason to go with 20 percent, I'd much rather round up.

Wait … what's this?

Oh, that's right, my finger is pointing down. That means my estimate so far is too *low*. So, if possible, in my next step I want to round in the *opposite* direction, up. That's my tiebreaker. I'm going to round 17.5 percent up to 20 percent, and because I've offset the previous rounding down by rounding up in this step, I'll hold my hand flat as a physical reminder that I don't need to adjust my estimate up or down. So now I have:

50 million x 20% x $300 (+ hand flat, indicating neutral)

Well, 50 million buyers times 20 percent is 10 million. Ten million times $300 is $3 billion. So let's compare our estimate to the actual answer to see how close we were. Once again, here's the original "precise" formula:

$$54 \text{ million} \times 17.5\% \times \$300 = \$2.835 \text{ billion}$$

Here's our formula based on rounded numbers:

$$50 \text{ million} \times 20\% \times \$300 = \$3 \text{ billion}$$

Our estimated computation was actually too high by only $165 million, which works out to a margin of error of + 5.8 percent. This is well within the +/- 20 percent margin of error that most consultants typically consider a "pretty good estimate." Based on the 20 percent margin, we could come up with an estimate as low as $2.3 billion or as high as $3.4 billion and still be considered by most consultants to have calculated a reasonable estimate.

This is the mental thought process you want to use when estimating numbers—round numbers intelligently in an offsetting fashion. If you round down to start, you want to round up next, and vice versa.

The discreet hand signals I use are as follows:

- Finger pointing down = estimate is too low
- Resting my hand flat on my leg = estimate is neutral
- Thumb pointing up = estimate is too high

Big-Picture Estimates

So far we have covered some of the skills needed to do estimations at the individual computation level. Now let's kick things up to a higher level and use these skills to estimate more-complicated figures such as market sizes.

Estimation Skill #3: Finding a Proxy

One of the big secrets to solving extremely complicated estimation questions is to find a useful proxy. What is a proxy? Merriam-Webster defines *proxy* as one who "acts as a substitute for another." In other words, the secret to solving complex estimation questions is to find some other number that mimics or somehow parallels the number we are looking to estimate. For example, let's go back to the estimation questions I encountered as a candidate:

- How many gallons (or liters) of gasoline does a typical filling station pump each week?

- Assume the year is 1980, and Motorola just invented a new technology called the cellular phone. The first three years of revenues for this technology have been terrible. As manufacturing costs and prices decline, what will sales for cellular phones be in 1985? Justify your estimate.

- How long does it take to relocate an average-size mountain 10 miles elsewhere using an average-size dump truck?

When interviewers asked me questions like these, my instinctive response was to panic, but I successfully answered these questions, passed the interviews, and got offers from all three firms that asked me those questions Oliver Wyman, McKinsey, and Bain. (Note: The interview process for these firms today differs from when I went through it. The examples that follow illustrate the range of difficulty you can expect when tackling a question like this. However, you should not use my personal experience as an indicator of which firms ask these types of questions in which interview round.)

As a candidate, I solved many of these estimation questions without explicitly realizing what I was doing. Only recently, as I've taught this topic, have I come to understand the key step that I, unlike many others, had performed instinctively. That step is finding the proxy.

When I first learned how to tackle estimation questions, most of the examples I found were about estimating a market: How many X are sold in America? I'd always been told to base my estimate on the size of the U.S. population. Without realizing it, I used population as a partial proxy for market size. Many other candidates ran into trouble anytime they got an estimation question that couldn't be solved based on the size of a population.

The key to solving estimation questions is not *to base your estimates on population size automatically. Instead, base your estimates on a relevant proxy (coincidentally, this is population much of the time).*

To find a relevant proxy, look at what you're estimating and ask yourself what proxies are correlated with or move proportionally with the number you're looking to estimate. Let's consider two of our three prior examples here.

Example 1

How many gallons (or liters) of gasoline does a typical filling station pump each week?

What factors correlate with how much gasoline a typical filling station pumps on a given weekday? Any thoughts? Here are mine:

- The average number of pumps each station has on-site
- The average number of cars that drive by, based on time of day (more cars during commuter hours, fewer cars during off-peak hours)
- The average percentage of pumps being used
- The average volume of gasoline pumped per car
- The average pump time per car

Example 2

Assume the year is 1980, and Motorola just invented a new technology called the cellular phone. The first three years of revenues for this technology have been terrible. As manufacturing costs and prices decline, what will sales for cellular phones be in 1985? Justify your estimate.

I nearly answered this tough question wrong. I'll walk you through my thought process, which you might find instructive. First, let me provide the context.

It was my Bain final-round interview. I had done well with all the other interviewers, and this was the last question, from the last interviewer, in the last round. I heard the interviewer ask the question, and I panicked.

I had never heard a question like this before, and I hadn't really grasped the concept of finding a proxy as an explicit step in the estimation process. Furthermore, based on personal knowledge, I knew the mobile phone would ultimately succeed. So in my head, I was thinking, *Don't shut down the mobile phone! It's going to work!* But how could I prove this based on what was knowable in 1980 as opposed to what we know today?

As I often do when I panic, I stalled for time! (I smiled calmly on the outside, but inside I was scratching my head.)

Here was my thought process: Clearly, sales will be a function of the size of the U.S. population. That's one factor, but it's not the primary factor, because the change in U.S. population size between 1980 and 1985 would probably be insignificant. I also knew that sales of this technology would skyrocket and be significant, so clearly population alone was not the best proxy. But what was?

As I thought about it further, I asked myself why people weren't buying cell phones in 1980. The main issue was the price; it was just so damned expensive. I'm sure I'm dating myself with this example, because many readers of this book might not yet have been born in 1980, but the early cell phones were incredibly costly.

So the first thing I said to the interviewer as I was thinking aloud about this problem was, "Well, I'm not a technology expert, but I know that most new technologies start off being very expensive because the manufacturer isn't making very many of them. At the same time, consumers are reluctant to buy a new technology that's a bit unproven and extremely expensive. So, as time progresses, technology costs will go down, prices will go down, and consumers will respond by buying more."

As I was saying this, I was thinking, *Yeah, I'm sure unit sales will go up as manufacturing costs and prices come down, but geez ... how fast will this happen? And how big will the unit sales increases be?*

Implicitly, I was trying to identify a good proxy for how quickly consumers would buy cell phone technology as prices fell. If prices fell by 20 percent, how much would unit sales increase? What would be the closest proxy?

That was the vague sentiment I had in my head, and I wish I had known enough to phrase it using these terms.

After thinking about it for a few moments, I got an idea and said, "It's not possible to know how quickly consumer demand will increase as prices decline for cellular technology, but maybe we can look at how quickly consumer demand has historically increased as prices declined for *other technologies*."

I explained this theory further. We have the first three years of sales data for cellular phones, and assuming we can get Motorola to estimate manufacturing costs at various product run sizes, we can triangulate the unit sales growth with the price-drop ratio for cellular technology. We could do this by comparing the first three years of sales for cellular technology with the first three years of sales for every other major new technology. As prices of fax machines dropped by 20 percent, for example, how much did unit sales increase? What about microwave ovens? Televisions? In essence, the adoption curve for cellular phones might mirror the adoption curve for other major new technologies.

That was the big insight that cracked the case for me, and much to my relief, the interviewer was more interested in my conceptual approach and didn't want me to calculate the actual number. She ended up offering me a job the next day.

In hindsight, I got lucky. I mean, how in the world is "an idea just popped into my head" a replicable process? I realize now that finding the proxy is *the* critical step in solving this and every other estimation question. Had I been consciously looking for the proxy, I'm certain my odds of answering a similar question would have increased and my performance would have been more consistent than it would have been had I relied on ideas popping into my head at the last second.

Estimation Skill #4: Identifying How Your Proxy is Imperfect

Once you've identified your proxies, you'll want to figure out what makes your proxies imperfect predictors of the number you're looking to estimate. For example, if we look at the gas station example, we know that how much gasoline a typical filling station dispenses is correlated to how many pumps the typical station has and what percentage of those pumps is used at any given time. So the number of pumps a station has is an "upper limit" constraint of how much gas a station can pump. If every pump is used 24 hours a day, seven days a week, then the total pumping volume will be determined by how many pumps that station has on the premises. We can be confident that this proxy sets the upper limit.

We know, however, that a gas pump will not be used all day long. Sometimes pumps sit idle, so the number of pumps is a useful but *imperfect* proxy. What you want to do is figure out *why* it's imperfect.

Here was my rationale: Car traffic peaks on local roads during commuter hours, which in the United States are roughly 7:00 a.m. to 9:00 a.m. and 4:00 p.m. to 6:00 p.m. The likelihood that most, if not all, of the pumps at a gas station are in use during those hours is quite high. During noncommuter hours, it's almost certain that fewer cars will be at the pumps.

This difference between peak and nonpeak driving hours (and hours when the filling station is closed for business) is the primary reason why the number of pumps alone isn't a perfect proxy.

Estimation Skill #5: Segmenting Estimates to Minimize Proxy Imperfections

Once you have a qualitative sense of what makes a proxy imperfect, segment your estimate into smaller, more precise sub-estimates. In the case of the gasoline-pumping example, I created three different estimates: one for peak driving hours (roughly four hours per day), one for off-peak driving hours (about 14 hours per day), and one for when the filling station was closed (six hours per day). Conceptually, my estimate looked like this:

Weekday gallons pumped = peak hours gallons pumped + off-peak hours gallons pumped + closed hours gallons pumped

Estimation Skill #6: Solving the Sub-estimates via Assumptions (aka Guesstimating)

Once you have segmented your estimates to minimize the imperfections caused by a particular proxy, solve each sub-estimate. You will typically be able to use a pen and a piece of paper (but not a calculator) to solve these computations.

Continuing with our prior example, we would start by estimating peak hour gallons pumped. If we break down that sub-estimate into its component parts, here's what the formula looks like:

Peak hours gallons pumped = (# peak hours) x (gallons pumped per peak hour)

Gallons pumped per peak hour = (total # pumps) x (% pumps utilized) x (# cars filled per hour) x (# gallons per car)

Now that we have a fairly detailed conceptual estimation framework, we guesstimate the numbers. Let's assume the average gas station has two islands. Each island has two stations. Each station has two pumps (one on each side of the island).

Total # pumps = 2 islands x 2 stations per island x 2 pumps per station = 8 pumps

Gallons pumped per peak hour = 8 pumps x (% pumps utilized) x (# cars filled per hour) x (# gallons per car)

The last time I was at a gas station during peak hours, most of the pumps were being used, so let's assume we have an 80 percent utilization rate during peak hours:

Gallons pumped per peak hour = 8 pumps x 80% utilization x (# cars filled per hour) x (# gallons per car)

When I fill my gas tank, it generally takes about a minute to park the car, swipe my credit card, and choose my type of gasoline. The actual pumping takes about four to five minutes, and it takes another minute to put the pump back, grab the receipt, and move my car. Let's say that, in total, it's a six-minute process. In a 60-minute time period, at six minutes per car, that means each pump can fill ten cars per hour.

Gallons pumped per peak hour = 8 pumps x 80% x 10 cars per hour x (# gallons per car)

My midsize car takes about 12 gallons to fill when the tank's completely empty. I know some cars take a lot more, and some of the smaller fuel-efficient cars take less. We also have to factor in those cars whose tanks are not completely empty when being filled. Considering these factors, let's assume the average fill per car is around ten gallons:

Gallons pumped per peak hour = 8 pumps x 80% utilization x 10 cars per hour x 10 gallons per car

Gallons pumped per peak hour = 640 gallons

Peak hours gallons pumped = (# peak hours) x (gallons pumped per peak hour)

Peak hours gallons pumped = (# peak hours) x 640 gallons

We previously established that there were about four peak hours per weekday:

Peak hours gallons pumped = 4 x 640 gallons

And let's round off the numbers for simplicity's sake:

Total gallons pumped during peak hours = 4 x 600 gallons = approximately 2,400 gallons

Now let's jump back up to our original conceptual estimation framework:

Weekday gallons pumped = peak hours gallons pumped + off-peak gallons pumped + closed hours gallons pumped

Weekday gallons pumped = 2,400 gallons + off-peak gallons pumped + closed hours gallons pumped

Further, we know that when the filling station is closed, it doesn't pump anything, so our real formula is:

Weekday gallons pumped = 2,400 gallons + off-peak gallons pumped + 0

Next, we need to solve the sub-estimate for off-peak gallons pumped. I'm a consultant by trade and training, so I'm inherently lazy (in other words, I like to be "efficient"). Rather than duplicate all the math I just did for peak hours, I'm going to use peak hours gallons pumped as a proxy to estimate off-peak gallons pumped. Let's recap what we now know:

4 peak hours per weekday = 2,400 gallons

Off-peak hours per weekday = 14 hours

Now let's estimate how much *less busy* a typical filling station is during off-peak hours compared to peak hours. I mentioned earlier that the typical island has all eight pumps running at roughly 80 percent utilization during peak hours. During off hours, I'm often the only person at an island, or sometimes one other person is there. So my guess is that the utilization rate is around 25 to 50 percent during off-peak hours, and we can simplify that by saying 40 percent of the pumps are utilized. This works out to be exactly half of the 80 percent utilization rate during peak hours. So let's go back to what we know:

4 peak hours per weekday = 2,400 gallons

That translates back to:

1 peak hour = 600 gallons

1 off-peak hour = 50% the utilization of a *peak* hour x 600 gallons

1 off-peak hour = 300 gallons

Total off-peak gallons pumped per weekday = 300 gallons per hour x 14 hours

Let's round the number and call it 300 gallons per hour for 15 hours. That works out to 4,500 gallons:

Weekday gallons pumped = peak hours gallons pumped + off-peak gallons pumped + closed hours gallons pumped

Weekday gallons pumped = 2,400 gallons + 4,500 gallons + 0 gallons

Weekday gallons pumped = 6,900 gallons

We would follow a similar process to estimate the gallons of gas pumped on weekend days and then add it to 6,900 to get our total estimate of how many gallons of gasoline a filling station pumps per week.

Practice Makes Perfect!

I hope this chapter has demystified estimation questions and shown you a process you can use to tackle these questions in your interviews. To be extremely proficient, you must practice the component-level math of large numbers and tackle estimation questions from top to bottom. To practice the component-level math of large numbers, including rounding, go here: www.caseinterviewmath.com.

I've posted a sample estimation question on my website. You can submit your answer and compare it to the answers of several hundred other people and to my answer key. This sample question and its answer key can be found here: www.caseinterview.com/jump/estimation.

PART THREE

Case Interview Fundamentals

Chapter 5

WHY CASE INTERVIEWS EXIST

REGARDLESS OF HOW the various types of case interview formats differ, the *skills* you need to tackle every case format are the same. Each format evaluates applicants' underlying consulting skills. If you demonstrate that you have mastered the skills that consulting firms want, you will do well in every type of case interview.

To appreciate why this is so and its implications for you, you must recognize why consulting firms do certain things during the recruiting process. Once you learn firms' underlying motivations, you'll better understand and even be able to predict what they look for in candidates.

I've helped many aspiring consultants get multiple job offers in consulting, and I often get thank-you emails from successful candidates (see www.caseinterview.com/success-stories). I call these successful candidates Future First Years (FFYs). They often report back to me on what advice from me they found helpful in passing the case interview. The information that follows is that advice.

Why Consulting Firms Do What They Do

Candidates often send me feedback about my explanations as to *why* consulting firms do what they do. Why do interviewers ask certain questions? Why do they use certain assessments? Why do they challenge your answers so aggressively?

This is important because *what* consulting firms do in the recruiting process changes yearly and sometimes from one interviewer to another. But *why* they do what they do has not changed in decades. If a candidate has enough interviews, he will encounter an exotic question, a new twist, or an extremely unusual case. It's impossible to predict when this will happen and therefore impossible to prepare for in advance. But if you understand the consulting firm's and the interviewer's motivations—what they're looking for and why—you'll find it's much easier to perform well in a situation you've never encountered before.

Case Interviews Simulate On-the-Job Experience

The case interview process is designed to find good consultants, and it does a surprisingly good job mirroring consultants' on-the-job experience. With that in mind, consider the following implications.

First, if you hate case interviews, you likely will hate the job. Being a consultant is like going through a case interview every day of your career.

Second, case interviews involve estimation questions because clients ask estimation questions all the time. Let's say a client is considering getting into the used-car sales market. That client will ask you, "Hey, (your name here), do you have any idea how big this market is?" So you say, "Well, there are 350 million people in America ..." And that's how it starts. I was asked plenty of estimation questions when I was a candidate, but once I started working at McKinsey, I ended up answering *more* estimation questions as a consultant than I ever did as a candidate.

Third, everything that happens in a case interview happens because it simulates some aspect of the on-the-job experience. When the interviewer asks you a random question in an interview, stop thinking like a candidate trying to impress the interviewer. Instead, think like a consultant: Ask yourself what you would feel comfortable saying to a client, knowing your firm's reputation is on the line—because it is.

Proving Yourself as a Consultant

The consulting team and firm must prove themselves early in their relationship with a client. When you start working with a new client, some individuals within the client organization may express skepticism about the value you and the consulting firm can bring. Your opinions don't count for much because you typically have less industry and business experience than the client does. So how can you prove your worth and be taken seriously?

- Ask clients thought-provoking questions they hadn't considered previously.
- Analyze data to discover new insights that clients haven't seen before.
- Develop data-supported conclusions (especially counterintuitive ones) that lead the client toward a different set of decisions.

Often the client or certain members of the client organization are looking to discredit you so they can get back to running the company. In that case, a semi-hostile client is looking for you to screw up somehow. The two most common screwups are the following:

- Offending a client (even junior clients and administrative staff) by being rude, arrogant, or dismissive
- Stating a conclusion you can't support with data

That's why the team has to be smart not only analytically but also interpersonally. It's also why many firms have adapted their recruiting processes specifically to find the candidates with the strongest interpersonal skills. Clients often interpret nervousness as a lack of conviction about a particular recommendation, which is why answering a case perfectly but nervously will get you rejected.

For example, if a consultant were to recommend nervously that the client lay off 2,500 employees, the client would second-guess the recommendation. Even if the recommendation were 100 percent correct, the client would sense some degree of hesitation, uncertainty, or reservation from the consultant based on *how* the message was delivered, not the content of the message itself.

As a result, consulting firm interviewers assess the level of confidence you project while solving a problem analytically. You don't need to be supremely confident and polished to pass a case interview, but you shouldn't be a complete nervous wreck incapable of stringing together a coherent presentation either.

As I mentioned, every aspect of the interview process happens for a reason, and most often that reason is to simulate some aspect of the on-the-job experience. This is the vital point to keep in mind as I cover in the next chapter the specifics of what interviewers are looking for and explain why they look for the things they do.

Chapter 6

WHAT INTERVIEWERS LOOK FOR AND WHY

IT'S IMPORTANT THAT you understand the psychology of why interviewers do the things they do. If you understand what they're thinking, it'll be a lot easier to impress them.

What I'm about to share is a *principle*—a timeless guideline you can apply to a wide range of situations. In comparison, a rule is something you're supposed to do in a specific situation.

Most candidates start the case interview learning process by seeking out rigid rules to follow. They think that if they can learn every interview format and every type of case question, they will be prepared.

But that's not a foolproof solution. Case interview formats and questions are constantly changing, and no matter how much you prepare, you'll likely encounter a type of case you've never seen. In fact, 20-year consulting veterans still learn from new situations they've never seen before.

That's not to say that preparation isn't useful and necessary. But in addition to preparing for your case interview, keep in mind a simple principle: Interviewers look for candidates who seem like colleagues already.

Act Like a Pro

As a case interviewer, I've interviewed strong candidates who've made me think, "Damn, this person's good." And at that moment, I began to think of those candidates as colleagues instead of job seekers. The tone of the interview switched from evaluative to collaborative. In essence, the candidate who stands out the most in an interview is the one who acts like a consultant already.

The more you learn about the on-the-job consulting experience and the interview process, the more you realize that the two aren't all that different. To me, a case interview is no different than a team meeting with the partner. (Again, if you don't like case interviews, you're really going to hate the job.)

Here's how the process works: Clients demand certain things of consulting firm partners, and partners expect their consultants to offer what the client demands. Consultants, who also serve as case interviewers, in turn demand these skills from the candidates they interview.

Once you learn how the job works, you'll find it much easier to navigate any interview situation, including times when you're surprised by a question, which happens all the time both in interviews and in working with clients.

How the Consulting Business Works

At the heart of every consulting firm are two groups of people: consultants and clients. Tension exists between these two groups because consulting firms charge very high fees, and clients don't like paying high fees.

Clients try to get consultants to charge less money by saying, "Well, does it really take eight weeks? Why don't you do it in six weeks?" or "Does it really take four people? Why don't you do it with three people?"

The client's budget often dictates how many people will be on the consulting team, so you can't add more people to the team if the client can't afford it. If you're working with a new client, you'll likely feel enormous pressure to over-deliver, which involves doing much more than you promised and billed for.

At McKinsey, we never discounted fees; we over-delivered, did extra work for clients for free, and worked harder. In an environment like that, you're under constant pressure to get more done with fewer resources, and that's just the way it is.

How Client Billing Works

In most consulting firms, each client and each of the client's projects has its own profit and loss statement (P&L). Each consultant on the team has two billing rates: one for what the client is billed for that consultant's contribution (typically an hourly or daily rate) and one for the consultant's "cost" to the firm (typically salary; benefits; other allocated expenses, such as rent, electricity, etc.). These rates are rarely published internally (or if published, not published very widely), but they exist to keep track of whether a client engagement is profitable.

When partners and managers look to staff their teams, they tend to look for the strongest contributors at every cost point—who provides the most value per dollar—in order to deliver higher-quality work at lower costs and maximum profit.

An interesting problem arises with brand-new first-year consultants, who often contribute *negative* value to an engagement team. More-experienced consultants must double-check at an extremely detailed level anything these consultants work on. Thus, the additional time required to manage new consultants largely offsets their contributions.

To "force" engagement teams to take on brand-new first-year consultants, some firms waive the first-year consultant's "cost" to the team's P&L. In other words, the engagement team can bill out that consultant to the client while showing a $0 cost on the engagement's P&L. (In these situations, the cost of the first-year consultant on his or her first assignment is billed to the training department.) This provides an incentive for client teams to take on free labor, "break in" the new consultants by mentoring them, and get some value out of them. This entire process, convoluted as it seems, exists in large part because first-year consultants have not yet proven their ability to solve problems independently.

The Value of an Independent Problem Solver

Let me share a story with you that illustrates why consulting firms value *independent* problem solvers.

In my third month at McKinsey, when I was only 22 years old, I was assigned to a client based in New York that had a small division in Cleveland, Ohio. The entire team, including me, was based in New York. All the other consultants on the team were married and had kids. Because I was a single guy, everyone said, "Let's send Victor to Cleveland!"

So I spent the next 18 months in Cleveland, working at the client site four days every week, with little on-site supervision. My manager went to Cleveland weekly, at most, for just one day, mostly to build client relationships and attend key meetings. The rest of the time I was on my own.

So, what was the project?

I worked with a $200 million division of a Fortune 500 company (small by Fortune 500 standards; the more senior consultants at McKinsey got divisions with $500 million to $900 million in sales) to figure out how to double sales and profits within three to five years. And that's all I was told; I had no other information to go on. In summary, I was told, "Hey, Victor, here's a plane ticket and an employee list. Go fly out to the client on your own, and figure out how to get another $200 million in revenue. See you in a few months."

This happens to consultants *all* the time. Plus, I had just 90 days of consulting experience then—not much more skill than what I had during the interview process.

When a consultant interviews you, she is wondering, *Can I drop you off with a division of a Fortune 500 company by yourself, with little to no supervision? Can you handle the client, solve its problems, and in the process make the firm look good?* That's what that consultant is *really* thinking, but most candidates don't appreciate this perspective.

The consultant's official role in the interview is to decide whether the firm should hire you. She is also thinking, *Do I want you on my team right now? Will my life get easier if you're on my team?* Phrased differently, that interviewer is asking herself, *Will you be an independent problem solver fairly quickly, or will I have to babysit you for the next two years of your career?*

My manager on the Cleveland project became a partner at McKinsey. Initially he tried to spend two days a week with me, probably to make sure I didn't screw up and embarrass him and the firm. Once he realized I could work independently, he left me alone, visiting at most only one day a week, so he could focus on doing partner-level activities—building relationships with the senior client, setting the stage to sell follow-on work, and networking with executives in sister divisions with which we weren't yet working.

His ability to do partner-level work was directly related to my ability (and the ability of the other consultants on the team) to be an independent problem solver. This is exactly why managers need independent problem solvers—their own career progress very much depends on it.

Doing as Little as Possible vs. Boiling the Ocean

As I mentioned previously, a routine problem in consulting is not having enough consultants to do all the work the client wants done. Clients want you to do as much work as possible for the lowest possible cost, whereas consulting firms want to charge as much as possible while doing as little work as possible and still delighting the client.

When you don't have enough resources, you also don't have the time, energy, or money to run every analysis you want. You end up having to make difficult choices in how you manage your time. In this context, many consultants use the phrase *boiling the ocean* to describe how *not* to prioritize your client work. As the metaphor goes, if you want one cup of hot water, there are two ways you can get it:

- Get one cup of water, put it on the stove, and boil it.
- Boil the entire ocean and then scoop up one cup of the boiling water.

Basically, the metaphor means that you can do as much or as little as possible to get the job done. In consulting, the latter is valued and praised.

So how does this relate to the case interview?

Interviewers tend to ask questions such as, "Given the client's main objective, what *key* information is needed to answer the client's question?" Many candidates use the "boiling the ocean" approach and list every little thing they think of, but managers in consulting teach new consultants *not* to do this, because there isn't enough time or staff to do everything.

Not surprisingly, when a candidate answers the question "What *key* information is needed to answer the client's question?" by listing *every* piece of information in the first three minutes of an interview, the interview is essentially over even before it has begun. The interviewer has to resist the urge to roll his eyes, because it would take far too long to get all the information the candidate suggests. At this point, the interview might as well be over because the decision has been made, but for the sake of politeness the interview continues.

Accurate Enough vs. Precisely Accurate

One trait about consulting that drives some people crazy is its general lack of precision. It drives engineers and scientists, who are accustomed to a high degree of precision in their chosen fields, particularly crazy.

If you talk to a civil engineer about how best to design a bridge, she will tell you precisely how thick the steel beams need to be, given the design specifications of the bridge. In contrast, if you talk to a consultant about the likelihood of something, he will typically give you a ballpark answer that deliberately has a margin of error of +/- 35 percent.

And why is this? You guessed it—the client! Most clients ask consultants yes/no or open-ended "what should we do?" questions, such as the following:

- Should we merge with our No. 1 competitor?
- Should we close our South America division?
- Should we enter the corporate accounts market segment?
- There's a price war in our industry, and we're losing a ton of money. What should we do?
- The introduction of XYZ technology has us deeply concerned about the future of our business. What should we do?
- Our two largest competitors just merged and are now bigger than us. What should we do?

In many cases, clients seek "directional" answers: "Yes, it's a good idea" or "No, it's a bad idea." Because of this, consultants typically don't have to make extremely precise math computations.

For example, a client might say, "It's worth it to us to enter XYZ market if we can generate at least $100 million a year within five years. Should we do it?" Let's say it takes a consultant a month to figure out that the XYZ market opportunity is likely a $200 million to $300 million opportunity for the client. The seasoned consultant would immediately stop the analysis and present the conclusion.

Let's further assume that it would take the project team another two weeks to figure out if the opportunity is worth $227.1 million or, say, $281.5 million. The person accustomed to precise math would be inclined to spend the extra two weeks to determine the more precise number. This is a mistake. The client did not ask how much the opportunity would be worth; the client wanted to know if it would be worth at least $100 million a year in five years.

In this example, being "accurate enough" gets the job done in four weeks, whereas being "precisely accurate" requires six weeks. As a consultant, you'll make decisions like this frequently, which is why interviewers screen out candidates who are uncomfortable with "accurate enough."

Often Right but Never Without Factual Justification

On my shelf sits the fantastically titled book *Often Wrong, Never in Doubt*, written by Donny Deutsch, an American celebrity entrepreneur. To me, the title represents a certain kind of business philosophy — *not* the philosophy of the management consultant. A more appropriate title for the consultant's version of the book would be *Often Right but Never Without Factual Justification*.

In consulting, you *always* pick and choose your words carefully, because you need to be able to back up anything you say. If you say a client should take X action, you'd better be able to explain why. If a client asks you a question you don't know how to answer, reply confidently that you do not have the facts to provide an accurate answer. If a client asks for your opinion, say you *suspect* X would be a good idea and then clarify, "But I don't have the facts to be 100 percent certain."

Notice that every statement can be supported factually, and every statement is said to the client confidently. If you don't know the answer, tell the client *confidently* that you don't know the answer.

Sure, this sounds uptight, but here's why it's important: When you say something, you are expressing not only your point of view but also your firm's point of view on the topic. Let's say you are a BCG consultant, and you say to the client that it should take X action. What the client hears is not that *you* think it should take X action; it hears that *BCG* thinks it should take X action.

The single biggest nightmare of partners at the top firms is some first-year consultant shooting off his or her mouth, saying something the firm cannot factually justify. After all, it makes the partners themselves look really bad. (Their second biggest nightmare is the new consultant being a jerk and offending the client.)

Choose Your Words Carefully

Why do interviewers nitpick every word you say during an interview? Because *clients* nitpick the same thing every day.

A consulting firm will interact with many people within a client organization. The primary client contact typically is friendly to the consulting firm, but some of the other client contacts may not be. Some resent the outside consultants. Some feel threatened that the outside firm will find their mistakes and make them look bad. Some even want to discredit the consulting firm.

These are the client contacts who nitpick what consultants say, which is why your choice of words even in an *interview* is important. If you say that something *always* makes sense for the client to do, be prepared to defend every possible situation in order to substantiate your argument. If the interviewer is in a particularly finicky mood and believes you made the wrong word choice, he might think up five different scenarios where your recommendation would not be correct, thereby forcing you to defend your point of view that the recommendation is *always* true.

Uptight? It sure is.

In this last example, it would've been much better to say, "Under most circumstances, the client should do X." It's much easier to defend "under most circumstances" than "always."

You would not believe how many 15-minute debates I've had with partners and managers over the relative merits of using a particular word over another in a presentation.

For example, I once had to convince a partner that the right recommendation to make to the client would be to sell off a $1 billion division. It took me 45 minutes to convince the partner of my logic and 15 minutes to determine whether the recommendation should be described as "necessary," "highly recommended," or "strongly recommended." The tendency was to make the case that the recommendation was "necessary," but we debated whether we had enough proof to substantiate that particular adjective.

Why do consulting firms do this?

It goes back to the principle of "often right but never without factual justification." There are two ways to stick to that principle: (1) Get more factual evidence to support your argument, which takes more time; or (2) soften the language of your argument and use the facts you already have.

Being Right vs. Being Right "Diplomatically"

Always pay attention to how you present your conclusions. Your analysis and conclusions aren't automatically "right." You need to communicate those recommendations diplomatically — in a way that's client-friendly.

Client friendliness is particularly important. Many businesspeople have excellent judgment and make good decisions (including many billionaires, incidentally), but many would make lousy consultants because they present their ideas too bluntly, without regard for how the other person receives the comment at an emotional level.

For example, making or stating conclusions without *showing and explaining* your work is not client-friendly. Let's say you go into a brain surgeon's office for the first time, and the surgeon does not have access to your medical history. The surgeon takes one look at you and says, "I have bad news: You're dying. I need to do emergency brain surgery in the next two hours or you won't live to see tomorrow morning. Let's go."

How would you feel?

If you're like most people, you'd say, "No way! There's no way you're drilling into my head. You haven't run any tests, done any analysis, or even examined me yet." Most people would have this reaction even if the surgeon happened to be correct in her incredible assessment. Maybe she saw a sign of a major life-threatening stroke. My point is, it doesn't matter if she's factually right unless she can explain *why* she's right to the patient, using terms the patient can understand.

The same idea applies to consulting. Clients do not accept factually accurate recommendations; they accept factually supported recommendations *they can understand*. Those last three words are worth gold, because they explain why interviewers look for good communicators, not just analytical problem solvers.

Interviewers highly value candidates who can think and communicate *linearly* (as opposed to jumping around in a scattershot way). They like candidates who say that A leads to B, and B leads to C, and therefore A leads to C. They tend to reject candidates who jump from concept A to U and then from F to T, even if these candidates arrive at the factually supported answer. The right answer is pointless unless a client can understand the process undertaken to get it.

In addition, if senior clients don't follow your argument, they might not tell you they're confused. Instead, they'll nod their heads as if they understand what you say but then not support your final recommendation—because secretly they didn't really "get it," and they don't want to appear "lost" in front of their peers.

If your clients don't follow your argument, guess whose fault it is? If you're a super-brilliant consultant but you make the senior client feel dumb because he couldn't follow your argument, guess what? Someone's getting fired from the relationship, and it won't be the client.

This principle applies to case interviews too. I recommend that you practice your communication skills as much as you do your technical problem-solving skills. I'll explain soon which communication skills to focus on, but for the time being, recognize the importance of these skills as a whole in a case interview, because quite often communication skills separate the candidates who get offers from those who make it to the final round but don't get offers.

The Airplane Test (aka Don't Be an Asshole)

One of the things you hear consultants talk about is the "airplane test," which is a way for an interviewer to judge your character by asking himself the following question: *Would I want to spend three hours sitting next to you on an airplane?* (Sadly, you often do spend a lot of time on airplanes with your colleagues.)

As the thinking goes, if the interviewer determines you don't pass the airplane test, then there must be something wrong with your interpersonal skills that would likely cause a problem with a client. That's the polite version of this story. The more blunt version can be summarized best by the title of a *New York Times* best-selling book written by a Stanford Graduate School of Business professor, called *The No Asshole Rule.*

As you might expect, the No. 1 rule to being a good consultant (or candidate) is *don't be an asshole.* I'm dead serious. No one likes to work with one, and that kind of behavior is just not client-friendly.

In consulting, you're often perceived as an outsider. Some client contacts perceive you as a distrusted, unwanted outsider. In situations like this, "tough" clients are looking—and even hoping—for you to be a jerk. That way they can discredit you and the firm, turn everyone else against you, and ultimately get you and your firm kicked out of the client organization. Don't give them any legitimate reason to do so.

McKinsey's consultants are sometimes perceived as being particularly arrogant. I don't think that was true most of the time (notice I didn't say it was *never* true—after all, that's a much harder position to substantiate). But because many McKinsey consultants were extremely accomplished, and often those accomplishments were mentioned early in an engagement to establish credibility, some people found McKinsey consultants arrogant.

Because that perception was so strong, I went out of my way not to be perceived as arrogant. Once I established my credibility, I tried to kill people with kindness and in some cases downplayed my accomplishments, even making a joke of them ("Yes, I did graduate from Stanford ... but don't hold that against me!").

In my first year at McKinsey, one of my engagement managers was a native German who transferred to the New York office. Germans have a reputation for prizing efficiency, and this engagement manager was no exception. In his first few months, he had difficulty adjusting to U.S. corporate culture, especially when dealing with clients in the Midwest, who like to chitchat.

My colleague didn't see the point of this "inefficient" conversation, generally did not participate in it, and simply asked for the data he needed. Of course, if you know Midwesterners, you know that some of them take offense at this kind of brisk treatment.

So I had to coach my manager, saying, "Come on, let's talk. Don't be an asshole. I know that chitchat is 'inefficient' conversation, but it's part of relationship building in U.S. business culture—especially in the Midwest. If you want their cooperation, you have to do it too." After about 90 days, my manager changed. He actually became chatty and made small talk. He stopped being an asshole and immediately became much more effective with U.S. clients.

Along these same lines, when you interact with the major consulting firms, your initial contact most often will be with a recruiting coordinator who plays an administrative role and does not participate in the client service functions of the firm. It's important that you treat this person like you would a future client—with a great deal of respect.

A recruiting coordinator can't get you a job offer, but she can make sure you don't even get an interview. (Similarly, when working with CEO clients, be extremely respectful of their administrative assistants. If you're a jerk, administrative assistants can make life much more difficult for you. If you treat them with the kindness and respect they deserve, they can use the clout of the CEO's office to get people in the organization to respond immediately to your requests.)

The Interviewer's Mind-Set

To understand the interviewer's mind-set, you need to understand a concept called *process excellence*. In the context of a case interview, process excellence is when a candidate is *consistently* able to follow a problem-solving process successfully over and over again. It's the idea of doing something the same way each time.

In a case interview, you are evaluated on two things: (1) your ability to follow a structured, analytical problem-solving *process*; and (2) your ability to reach the correct conclusions based on that process. Of these two areas, the *former* is much more important. Your ability to use a successful process consistently is substantially more important than is getting the right answer within the allotted time for the interview.

Interviewers perceive a candidate who gets a mostly correct but incomplete answer derived from a good process as more desirable than they do a candidate who gets the right answer but uses a poor and unrepeatable process. Interviewers see the latter as someone who just got lucky. Firms have multiple rounds of interviews because it's possible for a candidate to get lucky on one or two cases in a row, but it's very hard to get lucky on five to eight cases in a row.

When a candidate uses a consistent problem-solving process, it's only a matter of time before he gets the right answer. Your interviewer, who someday could be your manager, wants to feel confident that you can get the right answer, even if you aren't able to get it quickly. A manager can deal with a consultant who's consistently correct but a little slow. A manager can't deal with a consultant who's quick but inconsistent. It's easier to coach the former on how to be faster than it is to coach the latter on how to be more consistently accurate.

How Consultants (and Candidates Should) Think

When I was at McKinsey, the office was extremely busy one month. Consultants complained there was no downtime and vacation time between projects. Some of the partners expressed concern about this potential morale problem.

During a weekly Friday lunch, the head of the office held a discussion session to address the issues bothering the associates. During the session, a consultant suggested that office leadership eliminate all the snack foods in the entire office. At the time, the office was stocked with free soft drinks, potato chips, energy bars, cookies, and all the other things you eat late at night when you're starving.

The consultant made the suggestion for two reasons: one financial, the other health-related. He proceeded to give a very rigorous analysis to explain his suggestion. If each of the 1,000 office employees eats one cookie every other day, that's an average intake of 100 extra calories per person, per day. Add it up over the course of a year:

100 calories x 1,000 people x 252 working days in a year = 25,200,000 extra calories consumed

Given this calculation, the average New York consultant, independent of factors such as exercise, would gain about seven pounds per year, which would increase the firm's health care costs (self-insured). Over a ten-year period, health care costs would run the firm about $2 million—plus the expense of the food itself.

The head of the office responded humorously to this very serious suggestion, saying, "Obviously, we're not busy enough in this office."

I share this story to illustrate that this is *exactly* how consultants think. We can't *not* estimate or analyze anything we deem important. This example focused on analyzing an area that most people thought was pretty trivial, but the consultant's *process* was the exact process consulting firms value. It was linear, logical, and based on facts (and reasonable estimates of them); it used numbers to quantify; and most important, other people could follow the line of reasoning easily.

Interviewers assess how well you synthesize and communicate your big-picture conclusions. It's a hard skill to master. You have to shift your focus from the detail-oriented aspects of a business to the higher-level implications that need to be presented to the CEO.

Why Consulting Firms Value Strong CEO-Level Communication Skills

Many first-year consultants interview employees "lower down" in the client organization — the ones who spend all their time interacting with customers. The consultants ask, "What do you think is wrong with the company? What should we do about it?" Invariably, the consultants get an earful.

Consultants' numerical analyses of the frontline employees' theories quite often support those theories, proving that the people on the front lines know what's wrong — and have for some time. The consultants will then assemble a recommendation, *using supporting facts and analysis*, and present it to the client, often at a cost of millions of dollars.

Consulting firms are often criticized for this type of behavior. To an outsider, it seems like a client paid a lot of money to a consultant, only to have the consultant repackage the client's own insights in a different box. There is some truth to this criticism, but it misses an underlying point: Before the consultant entered the picture, many of these opinions were simply nebulous thoughts floating around the organization, and the CEO didn't know whose opinions to value. More important, the CEO didn't know which opinion to bet his or her entire career on.

The consultant often integrates these micro-recommendations into the big picture to show the client how they fit into the company's overall strategy, financial situation, and competitive position, thereby providing the client with enhanced *clarity* about the organization's problems and how to solve them. Integrating micro-recommendations into the company's big-picture vision and providing supporting facts and analysis for those micro-recommendations allow the consultant to instill greater *confidence* in the client about moving in a particular direction.

When a client has greater *clarity* about and *confidence* in a particular course of action, the client is much more likely to take action. For this reason, I'll argue that a consultant's high fees can be justified if the client follows through with a big decision the consultant recommended. So how exactly does a consultant convey clarity and confidence to a client?

One word: *synthesis*.

When a consultant delivers a well-synthesized recommendation, she usually has done two things well. First, she has put the recommendations *in context*. Instead of simply recommending that the client do X, a well-synthesized recommendation will recommend that the client do X because it will have ripple effects Y and Z, both of which are favorable. There may be concern about issue A, but the benefits of ripple effects Y and Z outweigh it. I call this process of highlighting all the ripple-effect ramifications of a particular course of action *connecting the dots*. Great synthesis connects all the dots, clarifying what likely will happen if the client follows—or ignores—the recommendation.

Second, the consultant has communicated with the CEO, using CEO-level language and an appropriate amount of detail.

In subsequent chapters, I provide examples of how to synthesize a case effectively. I urge you to use these "day in the life of a consultant"-type anecdotes to form a mental model of how a successful consultant thinks and acts. Think about that mental model as we transition to talking about the core problem-solving tools every aspiring consultant must master.

Chapter 7

THE CORE PROBLEM-SOLVING TOOLS

AS CASE INTERVIEW formats evolve, many candidates try to master the new formats. I always aimed to master the problem-solving tools that you have to use in any imaginable case format so I would be prepared for whatever happened in an interview. If you develop your problem-solving skills (as opposed to just your case interview skills), you will be able to deal with a wider range of problems in a case interview.

The core problem-solving tools I'll be sharing with you are the exact same tools consultants use in real life to serve clients. At McKinsey, I used these tools every single day, without exception. My friends from Bain, BCG, Monitor, A.T. Kearney, and others tell me they use these tools every day too.

Consultants use four tools to solve clients' biggest problems. You can use the exact same tools to tackle any type of case interview:

- Hypothesis
- Issue tree/framework
- Drill-down analysis
- Synthesis

I'll start by explaining each tool briefly and then cover each tool in depth in its own chapter.

Hypothesis

The word *hypothesis* comes from the scientific method, which a scientist uses to test an idea she has about what might be true in our world. "I *think* infections are caused by invisible germs we cannot see" is an example of a hypothesis. From here, the scientist makes intuitive guesses that form the basis for her hypothesis.

The next step in the scientific method is to construct an experiment to test this idea, or hypothesis, conclusively to determine if it is true. For example, in the pharmaceutical drug industry, you often hear the phrase *double-blind study*. In such a study, two groups of patients are compared: the control group, which receives a placebo (sugar pill) with no medical properties, and the experimental group, which receives the actual pill. If those who take the medication show the desired effect better or faster, scientists conclude that the pill works.

These three steps—hypothesis, experiment, and conclusion—are the same ones an aspiring management consultant should use to solve cases.

Before we address how consultants can use a similar process, let's expand upon how scientists use the scientific method. Viagra, which is used to treat erectile dysfunction, was originally hypothesized to be useful in treating high blood pressure. Researchers hypothesized that Viagra would reduce blood pressure in patients by dilating blood vessels.

In the experiment that followed, scientists discovered only modest blood pressure improvements in those male patients who took the drug. But those same patients reported having a remarkable sex life during the study, and thus a life-changing discovery was made. Based on this unexpected observation, scientists *revised* their original hypothesis to explicitly test this potential property of Viagra. The rest is history.

In science, the scientific method is an iterative cycle, with each phase based on a slightly different hypothesis born of the observations made in the previous phase. This iterative process captures the essence of the aspiring consultant's ideal problem-solving process.

Although the scientific method is the ideal approach for solving business problems, it's not the only one. Many successful business leaders solve complex business problems intuitively, based on gut instinct, but this approach is frowned upon in consulting, because even if intuitive recommendations are correct, proving them as such to clients is difficult.

Clients already have plenty of *opinions* about what to do; they don't need outside consultants to get opinions. Clients need *proof* as to which opinion is correct. Consulting firms have come to favor the scientific method approach when they need to prove a point, and as noted, this approach starts with the hypothesis.

Here's an example of a business problem and a hypothesis about what is causing it:

Interviewer: Company ABC's profit is down 20 percent.

Candidate: I'm going to hypothesize (based on some background information) that the client's industry is in a price war, which has caused the client's sales and profits to decline. To test this hypothesis, I need to know how the components of profits have changed since last year. In particular, I need to know how sales and expenses have changed since last year.

Interviewer: Sales have remained unchanged, and costs have increased by 20 percent.

Candidate: My conclusion is that my initial hypothesis seems to have been proven false. It looks like the client is facing a cost problem more so than a revenue problem. My next hypothesis is …

Notice how this hypothesis-experiment-conclusion process repeats itself. That's roughly how the dialogue would work. The first step is to state a hypothesis, and the second step is to decide how you will test your hypothesis using an issue tree, or framework.

Issue Tree/Framework

A scientist uses an experiment to test a hypothesis; a consultant uses an issue tree. An issue tree lays out a set of logical conditions that, if proven correct, prove the hypothesis correct. The term *issue tree* comes from the way such a logical structure looks—like a tree on its side—when diagrammed on paper:

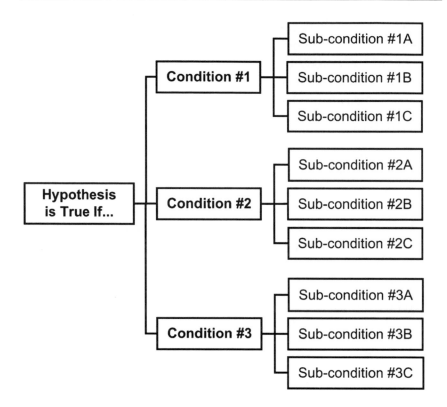

Figure 1: Issue Tree Diagram

Alternatively, you can think of an issue tree as a logical argument. Some people find the term *issue tree* confusing, so if you're one of these people, just substitute the term *logical argument* instead.

Attorneys use an issue tree structure when writing a legal brief. Your high school English (or native language) teacher used something similar when assigning an expository writing assignment in which you had to argue logically for a point of view.

The logic of an issue tree is as follows:

Hypothesis

- Condition 1
- Condition 2
- Condition 3

Phrased as a sentence, the issue tree says, "IF condition 1 is true and condition 2 is true and condition 3 is true, THEN the hypothesis must be true."

The sample issue tree above is a one-layer issue tree — one layer of conditions supports the hypothesis. A two-layer issue tree has two layers of conditions: one layer to support/validate the hypothesis and a second layer to validate the first layer. A two-layer issue tree looks like this:

Hypothesis

- Condition 1
  - Sub-condition 1A
  - Sub-condition 1B
  - Sub-condition 1C
- Condition 2
  - Sub-condition 2A
  - Sub-condition 2B
  - Sub-condition 2C
- Condition 3
  - Sub-condition 3A
  - Sub-condition 3B
  - Sub-condition 3C

In the two-layer issue tree example above, Condition 1 is proven true if Sub-conditions 1A, 1B, and 1C are proven true.

Frameworks as Issue Tree Templates

A framework is essentially a template based on a commonly used issue tree. Because consultants tend to see similar problems among many different clients, some have developed frameworks to deal with these frequently occurring problems.

For example, many clients experience declining profits. To address this situation, many consultants use what I call the *profitability framework,* which breaks down a company's profits into its component parts: revenues and expenses. Revenues are further broken down into their component parts: product prices and quantities of product sold. A similar breakdown is used for costs.

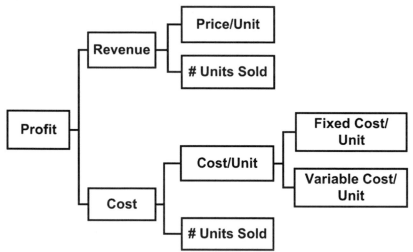

Figure 2: Profitability Framework Diagram

In the profitability framework, the logical construct happens to be quantitative in nature and uses a mathematical equation to solve profitability problems. For example:

$10 million in profits = $20 million in sales - $10 million in costs

An issue tree or framework structure applies to not only mathematical conditions but also conceptual ones. For example, if your hypothesis is "We should eat Mexican food for dinner," your logical argument structure might be:

Eating Mexican food for dinner is the optimal choice

- Culinary benefit: We like the food
- Financial benefit: It's affordable
- Social benefit: Our friends like Mexican food too and will accompany us

You can argue whether the three conditions I've chosen provide a valid logical argument. Assuming the structure is valid, the logic says that if all three conditions are proven true, then our hypothesis is true. If we can confirm that everyone in our group likes Mexican food, the food costs less than $X per entrée, and our friends would join us if we decided to eat Mexican food for dinner, then logically the hypothesis is valid and thus becomes our conclusion: Yes, we should eat Mexican food tonight.

Sometimes interviewers complain that poorly performing candidates either don't use an issue tree at all or choose conditions for their argument that aren't logical. They also complain that many candidates rely too much on issue tree templates (frameworks) rather than think critically about the specific hypothesis at hand and devise a *logical* issue tree (whether it's a template or otherwise). Many candidates use the most *convenient* issue tree that comes to mind (usually a framework that seems topically similar), even if it isn't necessarily logical for the specific hypothesis at hand.

Consultants refer to the process of devising logical arguments or issue trees to test their hypotheses as *problem structuring*. So if an interviewer tells you that your problem structuring is weak, it means one of two things: (1) You forgot to state your issue tree early in the interview, or (2) your issue tree isn't logical. If the interviewer tells you your issue tree isn't logical, it means your argument has a logical flaw—either the conditions you chose aren't logical for the specific hypothesis at hand or you omitted a key condition.

We'll cover issue trees and frameworks in more detail later, but for now, just recognize their role in the case interview and how the entire rest of the case centers on getting the issue tree right.

Drill-Down Analysis

Once you have a logical argument, you'll need to analyze the data to prove or disprove each condition of the hypothesis. I call this *drill-down analysis* because you start at the top of your issue tree and drill down through all the logical branches and sub-branches, gathering data to factually prove or disprove that branch (or sub-branch).

When you do drill-down analysis properly, you reach a logical dead end—a point at which you have clearly proven all conditions within a branch and can logically conclude that a particular branch of your argument is valid. A logical dead end also exists when you've proven a particular branch false and *invalid*. When the latter occurs, you have effectively disproven your hypothesis, so you must consider a new one. As part of this process, you will often go back to your revised hypothesis and use drill-down analysis to analyze the remaining branches of your issue tree (assuming the branches are still relevant and have not been modified due to your revised hypothesis).

Drill-down analysis is essentially a process of elimination. You drill down one branch of analysis, disqualifying or qualifying its relevance, which very much simulates the iterative problem-solving approach typical of consulting and case interviews.

If you're doing the analysis correctly, you are *constantly* drilling down one branch, discovering it's not valid, revising your hypothesis (and often the branches of your issue tree), and then drilling down an entirely new branch. You do this over and over, all day long, in both consulting and case interviews. Drill down, pull up, revise the hypothesis, restructure the issue tree, drill down again ... lather, rinse, repeat.

This process-of-elimination approach ends once you've proven every branch of your issue tree (which may have been revised several times) and can logically conclude that your most recent hypothesis must be valid. At this point, you're ready to use the last tool in your problem-solving tool kit: synthesis.

Synthesis

Synthesis involves stating your conclusion in a way that

- Tells the client *what to do*

- Tells the client *what you discovered* and *what it means*

- Couches your recommendation *in the context* of the overall business, not just in terms of the single decision the client asked you to assess

To pass case interviews, you must synthesize and communicate your discoveries in the way C-level (CEO, COO, CFO, etc.) clients prefer those discoveries to be communicated. Your communication must be concise, integrate detailed analysis in view of the big picture, and be action-oriented.

Many analytically strong candidates, including those with PhDs in engineering and the sciences, who are new to the case interview process can solve a case effectively up until the synthesis stage. These candidates understand the logical and quantitative aspects of the case clearly, but they sometimes find that explaining their discovery concisely to an interviewer (or client) can be challenging.

Most candidates close a case by summarizing the steps they took to arrive at the conclusion, which typically looks like this:

- What I learned #1
- What I learned #2
- What I learned #3
- What I learned #4
- What I learned #5

Essentially, case interview beginners instinctively want to *list* every fact they discovered during the case. For example, someone using this structure might say:

- Sales are down 20 percent in the Northeast.

- Your competitors have a manufacturing cost advantage you can't match.

- The Fortune 500 account customer segment is growing the fastest.

The problem with this approach is that it's difficult for the client to understand what all this data *means* and what the client should *do* about it. This is *not* the preferred way to synthesize. The preferred method uses the following structure:

- What client should do
  - Why client should do it—Fact #1
  - Why client should do it—Fact #2
  - Why client should do it—Fact #3
- Restate what client should do based on these facts

In the ideal synthesis, you *start* your communication by stating what the client should *do*. I call this an *action-oriented conclusion statement*. The following are examples of this type of statement:

- You need to shut down the Eastern region factory.
- To achieve your financial goals, you must enter the XYZ market immediately.
- You should lay off 3,000 employees.
- You should invest the $100 million needed to build a new factory.

After making your action-oriented conclusion statement, lay out the rationale for your recommendation by citing key facts to support it. Quite often the structure of your closing argument will mirror your final issue tree structure.

We'll cover the details of how to synthesize your conclusions properly in an entire chapter devoted to the subject, but for now you should familiarize yourself with the roles these four tools play in the case interview. Learn them well, because you'll be using them a lot, and if you're not using all of them a lot, you're probably doing something wrong! So here they are again:

- Hypothesis
- Issue tree/framework

- Drill-down analysis
- Synthesis

You'll use these four problem-solving tools over and over again in every case interview (and client engagement). Sometimes you'll use these tools in a team environment, as in a group case interview, while other times you'll use them in a written exam, as in a written case interview. In some cases, you may be asked to use the first three tools to prepare and then give a presentation to the interviewer, as in a presentation-based case interview. In other situations you'll go through the four tools with the interviewer, as in an interviewer-led case interview.

Regardless of the format of the case interview, you will use these core tools repeatedly. In the next four chapters, I outline everything you need to master these four tools. Once you do, you'll be prepared for virtually any type of case format or question.

Chapter 8

THE HYPOTHESIS

NOW THAT YOU have a basic understanding of a hypothesis and its role in solving client problems, let's focus on the subtle aspects of using a hypothesis effectively in case interviews.

Many case interview beginners find it unnatural to decide upon and verbally state a hypothesis at the beginning of a case. They think it's counterintuitive to make an educated guess *before* gathering data or doing analysis. After all, isn't it backward to state a conclusion at the very beginning? Shouldn't analysis precede and inform the conclusion?

Analyzing everything first takes an enormous amount of time—time you don't have in a case interview. In a client engagement, you have a set number of weeks to deliver a recommendation, but in a case interview you typically have only 30 to 40 minutes either to complete the case or to get within a step or two of the finish line.

When you attempt to analyze everything, it's entirely possible you won't make any *definitive* conclusions by the time you've completed 50 percent of the analysis. Sure, you've gathered a lot of data, but you haven't necessarily made any progress in truly *understanding* what's going on.

In contrast, when you take a hypothesis-driven approach, your initial hypothesis often is not correct, but you're able to determine quickly and with extremely high confidence what is *not* true. This shortens the problem-solving process by *reducing the range* of possible conclusions.

When to State Your Hypothesis

Now that you understand the rationale for using a hypothesis, let's clarify *when* you should use it. The consensus among interviewers is that a hypothesis should be used *early* in a case interview, though interviewers are divided regarding precisely how early.

One school of thought says you should state your hypothesis immediately at the opening of a case. The minute the interviewer explains the case background, state your hypothesis and move on to the other problem-solving tools.

The other school of thought says you first take one to four minutes to ask some background questions about the client's situation and then state your hypothesis. Interviewers in this camp argue that stating a hypothesis when you have no background information seems overly formulaic and robotic.

As a candidate, I belonged to the latter school of thought, and out of more than 60 cases, I never stated a hypothesis within the first 30 seconds. That said, I didn't wait more than four or five minutes to state a hypothesis.

As a former case interviewer, I don't care whether a candidate states a hypothesis in the first or the fifth minute of the case, as long as she states one.

You can ask a few background questions before stating your hypothesis, but if you take this approach, you risk forgetting to state a hypothesis at all. Sometimes when you get a really fascinating case, you'll be so intrigued by it that you'll ask question after question and perhaps forget to actually state a hypothesis. Again, it's perfectly fine to ask a few background questions before you state a hypothesis, but don't forget that all-important first step.

Five-Minute Hypothesis Rule

One of my blog readers emailed me following his interviews at BCG and A.T. Kearney:

> Going through your prep materials, I realized that understanding the problem through some cursory data gathering was the key to laying out a sound structure for the case ... such an approach was received favorably by most interviewers, as it gave a feeling that I was according the respect that the individual case in

question deserved rather than a standard case interview framework or structure being force-fitted to every case.

My trusted personal rule is to consider what works with clients and then do that with interviewers. Why? If you meet client team members for the first time and tell them your hypothesis as to what is wrong with their company *before* you ever ask them any questions, they look at you with suspicion and distrust. It's akin to the brain surgeon in the earlier example who takes one look at you and says, without having run any tests, that you need emergency brain surgery.

You want to delay stating a hypothesis long enough to establish some basis for it but not so long that you forget to state it at all. As I mentioned, it's easy to ask a few questions, be surprised by the answers you get, ask a few more questions, and then realize that 20 minutes of your 30-minute interview have gone by without you having stated your hypothesis.

Several candidates forgot to state a hypothesis during mock interviews in my Look Over My Shoulder program (www.caseinterview.com/jump/loms). In the debriefing sessions, these candidates had difficulty determining where to draw the line between asking a few initial clarifying questions and asking too many. I asked these candidates about this. They all said they knew what a hypothesis was and that they were supposed to state one, yet two out of three did not do so.

Stress is to blame here. It's easy to understand what you're supposed to do, but doing it under real-world conditions and stress can be difficult. This is why I emphasize not just taking notes on how to do a case but also devoting as much time as possible to practicing your case interview skills.

My discussion with these candidates prompted me to create a rule for a specific time within which you should state your hypothesis. I call it the *Five-Minute Hypothesis Rule*.

If you have not stated a hypothesis by the fifth minute of a 30-to-40-minute interview, you're probably at serious risk of forgetting to state a hypothesis entirely. Regardless of what you have discovered by the fifth minute of the interview, I suggest that you state your best-guess hypothesis right then, lest you forget to state a hypothesis at all.

If you plan to use a deliberately delayed hypothesis statement, let the interviewer know by saying something like, "Before I state a hypothesis, I'd like to ask a few clarifying questions." The interviewer will know you intend to state a hypothesis and won't think you forgot. But if you do forget, the interviewer can remind you of your original intention, and this incurs less of a penalty than does forgetting entirely.

The Five-Minute Hypothesis Rule will not work in a certain type of case interview. Most McKinsey offices use an interviewer-led, or "command and control," format that artificially breaks up a case into semi-independent sections. The whole case interview consists of about five sections, each lasting about six minutes and focusing on a different aspect of the same case. This type of interview jumps from one part of the case to another in no particular order.

In one section of this type of interview, the interviewer will ask for your intuition about the case, which is basically just another way of asking for your hypothesis. The hypothesis and its corresponding issue tree are a distinct *prescheduled* step for this interview format. During the specific time allotted for the hypothesis and issue tree, you must define both items, and you will not have the chance to revisit this step later in the interview.

Whether it's better to state a hypothesis too early or too late, the final word is that it's far worse to be too late. The latter will get you rejected, but the former by itself won't.

Chapter 9

THE ISSUE TREE

JUST LIKE A scientist devises an experiment to test a working theory about a disease, you need to determine how to test your client's problem or challenge. Interviewers commonly call this step *problem structuring*. When a candidate cannot find a clean, logical, definitive way to test a hypothesis, interviewers often say the candidate has poor problem-structuring skills.

To test a hypothesis, you need to create an issue tree, which identifies the key issues that, once known, will conclusively determine whether a hypothesis is true.

The term *framework* is used more often than is *issue tree* in case interview circles. A framework is an issue tree *template* – an initial structure for common business problems. A framework serves as a starting point for an issue tree and should be customized for every case.

For example, many clients' companies lose money, and typically one of a dozen or so common reasons can explain why. Thus, one commonly used issue tree deconstructs profits into component parts, enabling you to analyze each component to identify the root, or underlying, cause of the profitability problem. Because this is a somewhat standard analysis, we call this the *profitability framework*.

- Issue tree: A logical argument or structure designed to test the validity of a hypothesis
- Framework: An issue tree template used to solve common business problems (must be customized on a case-by-case basis)

The Structure of an Issue Tree

As noted in Chapter 7, the term *issue tree* comes from the way such a logical structure looks – like a tree on its side – when diagrammed on paper:

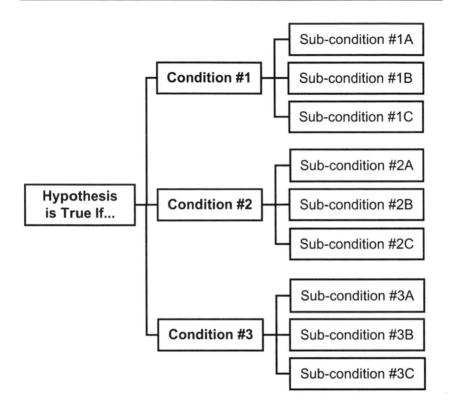

Figure 3: Issue Tree Diagram

An issue tree, which is also sometimes called a logic tree, is a logical argument, the validity of which can be tested via data.

Stated differently, the logic of an issue tree and a hypothesis is analogous to the "if/then" statement common in logic arguments and proofs:

- Issue tree branches = if
- Hypothesis = then

If these three factors (Branch 1, Branch 2, Branch 3) are true, *then* the hypothesis is true. The if/then construction provides a clear, logical structure that can be proven or disproven with factual data. This is the essence of problem structuring using issue trees—you make a logical argument based on the hypothesis that can be easily validated with concrete data.

A well-structured issue tree passes the following three validity tests:

- Your hypothesis
- The McKinsey MECE test
- The Victor Cheng "conclusiveness" test

Issue Tree Validity Test #1: Your Hypothesis

Most candidates obsess over memorizing a few key frameworks and end up focusing on the wrong things. The framework is a commonly (but not exclusively) used tool. The more important skill is the ability to take your hypothesis and create an issue tree (or customize a standard framework) that will logically test *your* hypothesis in this *specific* case. A framework is a commonly used issue tree to test common hypotheses. But a framework has limitations—it does not cover all hypotheses for all possible situations.

Many candidates jump into a framework without having stated a hypothesis, which interviewers find ridiculous: How can you create a structure to test a hypothesis if you haven't even stated a hypothesis?

Interviewers commonly tell such candidates that their problem structuring was weak or their approach wasn't hypothesis driven (they used a framework in a "going through the motions" way, without the *specific intent* to test a hypothesis). Interviewers give this type of feedback all the time, and many of my readers email me asking how to interpret it. Irritated interviewers express frustration with candidates who use frameworks but don't really grasp *why* they're using them.

The *only* reason you use a framework or issue tree is to test a hypothesis!

Remember this. I know many readers of this book will either forget this point or simply not apply it in practice despite the emphasis I've put on it.

Issue Tree Validity Test #2: The McKinsey MECE Test

The issue tree has both a simple name and a fairly simple function: In considering a decision (your hypothesis), the issue tree lists the *most relevant* factors you must consider in making that decision. That said, a well-structured issue tree should pass something called the *mutually exclusive, collectively exhaustive* (MECE) test, developed largely at McKinsey & Company, which provides a way to categorize any type of information.

In the context of consulting and case interviews, the MECE principle describes how decision-making factors should be categorized in order to minimize confusion and ensure problem-solving thoroughness. Specifically, all the information should be grouped into discrete categories, with no overlap between categories (mutually exclusive), and all the categories added together should cover all possible options (collectively exhaustive).

We can group customers into categories (which consultants call *customer segments*) in accordance with the MECE principle or not. Customers grouped by hobbies, for example, do not follow the MECE principle because an individual customer can belong to more than one hobby category. In contrast, customers grouped by age pass the MECE test because no individual can belong to more than one age category (mutually exclusive), and the age categories cover the entire population (collectively exhaustive).

The MECE principle can be applied to groups of related items, such as customers in different age brackets, and can also be used to group quantitative data. For example, the following formula is a MECE framework:

$$Profits = revenues - costs$$

It very simply communicates that one of two things must happen to increase profits: (1) Revenues must increase, or (2) costs must decrease. The components of revenues (typically unit pricing and units sold) do *not* appear in the cost category (and vice versa). As such, this formula fulfills the mutually exclusive criterion of the MECE test.

In addition, if you combine all the factors (both revenues and costs), the combination of all categories fully explains the cause of a change in profits; no other factor is missing. Thus, this categorization fulfills the collectively exhaustive criterion of the MECE test.

The MECE principle can also be applied to conceptual data. For example, let's say a client asks, "Should I enter the XYZ market?" You might say there are two possible categories of factors to consider in analyzing this decision: (1) financial factors, and (2) nonfinancial factors. Every possible reason for or against this decision can be grouped into one of these categories. Items that are financial in nature cannot appear in the nonfinancial category, and vice versa, so the categorization structure is mutually exclusive.

In addition, if you combine *all* the financial *and* nonfinancial factors, no other reason exists as to why entering the XYZ market is a good or a bad idea. Both categories together cover *all* the possible factors to be considered, so this categorization is collectively exhaustive. Because both categories are mutually exclusive *and* collectively exhaustive, this categorization passes the MECE test.

Let's apply the MECE test to another structure:

- External factors (market factors such as customers, competitors, industry regulation, etc.)
- Internal factors (the client's internal operations)

As in the previous example, any factor that is internal by definition cannot be considered an external factor, so the structure is mutually exclusive. In addition, because all factors are either external or internal, both categories combined are collectively exhaustive. As a result, this structure passes the MECE test.

When you create an issue tree or modify an issue tree template, the structure should as closely as possible adhere to the optimal MECE structure. Being 100 percent MECE isn't always possible, practical, or efficient, so in those cases it's sufficient to be as MECE as possible. Let me give you some examples.

In a math-driven issue tree such as the profitability framework, the issue tree can maintain its MECE structure through multiple layers:

- Profit = revenue - costs (that's MECE)

- Costs = fixed costs + total variable costs (that's MECE too)

- Total variable cost = cost per unit x number of units sold* (that's MECE too)

  * Technically speaking, it should be the number of units *manufactured*. In practice, we interchange units manufactured and units sold because at a *strategic* level the difference is considered negligible (unless information exists that suggests otherwise).

Issue trees can also categorize conceptual data where the relationship among categories can be described in a mathematical formula. For example, many clients ask consultants to advise them on whether they should introduce a new product. In this case, consultants commonly consider factors related to the client's customers, its competitors, the company, and the product itself. So the issue tree structure looks like this:

Hypothesis: Introducing XYZ product makes sense.

- Favorable customer factors
- Favorable competitive environment
- Favorable company operations factor
- Favorable aspects related to the product

This structure isn't 100 percent MECE. Sure, customer factors, competitor factors, and company factors are fairly mutually exclusive, but the product factors could overlap with competitor factors and company factors. You could cover products twice—once under competitors and once under company. But part of the insight in considering a product introduction strategy comes from comparing the client's product to its competitors' products.

Issue Tree Validity Test #3: The Victor Cheng "Conclusiveness" Test

The final test of a valid issue tree is to ensure that using it will produce relatively conclusive results. What I mean by this is that the following statement should be true about your issue tree structure: *If* all the branches of the issue tree turn out to be true, I can't imagine a scenario in which the *opposite* of my hypothesis would be true.

This qualitative test forces you to consider if you've missed any important factors that should be included as a branch of the issue tree. In addition, it forces you to remove any factors that do not conclusively prove or disprove your hypothesis (or at least substantially improve the conclusiveness of your hypothesis). Here are some examples:

Hypothesis: Apple should enter the tablet market with its iPad product.

- Customer — The future size of the market is potentially very large, with extremely strong growth prospects.
- Competition — No competition exists, providing a competitive vacuum.
- Company — We have a unique competitive advantage in product design and could bring to market a unique product in this segment.
- Return on investment — The potential financial benefit likely will outweigh the research and development costs.

Keep in mind that an issue tree is designed so that you can challenge and attempt to disprove a specific hypothesis. In this case, it's easier to prove a hypothesis that you know turns out to be true. For our purposes, however, we could just as easily have used the following hypothesis and issue tree instead:

Hypothesis: Apple should *not* enter the tablet market with its iPad product.

- Customer—Market demand does not exist today, and nothing indicates that demand will ever exist.
- Competition—Competition in this market is intense and saturated.
- Company—We have no competitive advantage in product design and would be incapable of bringing a unique product to market.
- Return on investment—The research and development costs would massively outweigh aggregate future revenues.

These two examples prove that it's not all that critical whether the hypothesis is "for" or "against" a particular decision. What is critical is that each branch has something concrete that could be challenged with factual data, each branch tests a distinct aspect of the argument separate from the other branches (is mutually exclusive), and all the branches combined cover the entire range of key issues (are collectively exhaustive).

The structure of the two issue trees above indicates that *if* future customer demand is favorable, *if* no competition exists, *if* Apple can produce a unique offering, and *if* the return-on-investment profile is favorable, *then* entering the tablet market with the iPad would be a good idea.

Using my conclusiveness test, you'd want to ask yourself, "Can I imagine any scenario where entering the iPad market would be a *bad* idea (the *opposite* of my hypothesis), assuming future demand *is* favorable, competition does *not* exist, Apple *can* produce a unique product, and the return on investment *is* attractive?"

Conversely, you could use the thoroughness test to ask yourself, "*If* all four of those factors—customer demand, competition, company, and return on investment—are *unattractive*, can I imagine any scenario where entering the market would be a *good* idea?"

Now, let me show you a counterexample. Let's take our issue tree above and modify it so it fails my conclusiveness test. In particular, let's modify the competition branch. Instead of having our branch on competition state that no competition exists, let's rephrase it as "Amazon.com's future tablet product will likely be priced higher than our product."

In essence, the issue tree now argues that, assuming a competitor's product is priced higher than our product, entering the market seems favorable. But before we use this issue tree structure, we have to ask if this logical structure is conclusive.

We can test for conclusiveness by taking the same "if" conditions and comparing them to the *opposite* of our original "then" hypothesis statement. In other words, "Assuming that Amazon's price for any future product would be higher than Apple's, can we imagine a scenario where entering the market would be a bad idea?"

Several scenarios come to mind for me. For example, maybe Amazon has a higher-priced product, but what about HP or BlackBerry or some other competitor? Maybe all the other competitors have lower prices, but Amazon has a higher one. Using the Amazon example in the if/then statement results in low conclusiveness for the issue structure.

We can also test for conclusiveness by reversing the "if" condition to see if it could possibly still support the same "then" hypothesis statement.

For example, we could say, "Assuming the price of Amazon's future product is *lower* than Apple's, can we imagine a scenario where Apple could still do well in the tablet market?"

The short answer is yes. Maybe the Amazon product costs less *and* does less. In this case, Apple could still win. So again, this if/then structure using Amazon results in low conclusiveness for the issue tree structure.

You want to run this conclusiveness test on *each* branch of your issue tree (to see if perhaps that branch should be defined differently or perhaps excluded entirely) and on your issue tree as a whole (to see if you missed something that should be included in one of the issue trees).

The Importance of Issue Tree Validity and Strong Problem Structuring

If your issue tree (or your framework) does not pass these three tests, then the validity of your issue tree declines dramatically. When you start a case with poor problem structuring, it's nearly impossible to fix it later.

This topic around issue tree validity (which interviewers describe as "good problem structuring") is so critical that I strongly recommend you reread the paragraphs above several times until you grasp the concept.

The Framework—A Commonly Used Issue Tree

Many clients struggle with the same business problems: How do we improve profits? Grow sales? Enter a new market? Because clients tend to face similar problems, consultants (and by proxy, candidates) address these same problems with many different clients. Some consultants have developed frameworks to deal with these frequently occurring problems.

Case interview beginners use the term *framework* far more often than they do *issue tree*, and I believe this is a mistake. An issue tree can be used to structure *any* business problem, so it provides the maximum flexibility to cover the widest range of problems. In contrast, a single framework covers just one (somewhat common) business problem.

I think the emphasis on frameworks, at the expense of issue trees, is misplaced, because during interviews a candidate commonly will be asked to deal with a business problem that is *not* covered by a standard framework or one that has an unusual twist.

The Curse of the Framework Robot

A candidate who has memorized a few frameworks but lacks an understanding of the underlying issue tree process will struggle with applying this tool effectively. I call this type of candidate a *framework robot* because he, like a robot, mechanically uses a previously memorized framework but cannot think critically as to whether that framework is relevant to a particular case situation. The framework robot attempts to force a case to fit within a framework he knows, even though that framework was never designed to solve that type of case.

This mechanical approach probably is the single biggest complaint interviewers have about candidates. They can't stand when a candidate states a previously memorized framework that has absolutely, positively nothing to do with testing the hypothesis. (This assumes the candidate actually has a hypothesis. Incidentally, the lack of a hypothesis is probably the next biggest complaint interviewers have about candidates.)

This is not to say you shouldn't familiarize yourself with a handful of frameworks. In fact, I cover several of my favorite frameworks in the next section of this book. But I don't want you just to memorize frameworks without understanding the underlying issue tree structure. If you understand the underlying structure, you won't be stuck when you have a hypothesis that simply cannot be adequately tested by a standard framework. Instead you'll be able to

1. Recognize the situation.
2. Notice where the framework falls short.
3. Create a customized issue tree (that perhaps incorporates parts of the standard framework) to test the hypothesis logically.

My students who get the most job offers routinely are proficient in this "create and then test the hypothesis" way of thinking. Sometimes this involves using a framework, and other times it requires using a custom issue tree. When you're adept at problem structuring, you can switch effortlessly between the two approaches, mixing and matching components of each, as appropriate, to test your hypothesis logically.

Notice how frequently in these past few pages I've used the word *logic* and logical constructs such as if/then. The case interview is very much a logical and critical-reasoning evaluation process; it is *not* a memorization test.

Candidates who memorize frameworks without ever learning the critical-reasoning process behind them tend to struggle with the case interview, whereas candidates who grasp the logical critical-reasoning process tend to do well, even if they haven't memorized many frameworks.

Keep these subtle but critical distinctions in mind as we cover frameworks in more detail throughout the rest of the book.

The Relationship Between Hypothesis and Issue Tree (or Framework)

I receive many emails asking if I have a framework for some unusual kind of case—for example, one involving a nonprofit, human resources organization design, manufacturing process improvement, or IT vendor selection. Although I focus on strategy consulting cases, people want to know if I have a framework for these unusual cases, mostly because of a dearth of information online about how to solve them.

I can tell just by how someone phrases one of these questions whether she grasps something very fundamental about how to approach solving a case. People seem to be obsessed with picking the "right" framework. This obsession is misplaced.

When I get such a question, my instinct is to ask two questions, the answers to which will provide the "right" framework for *any* case—strategy, human resources, manufacturing, technology, or otherwise:

1. What is your hypothesis?
2. What data do you need to disprove it?

Sometimes it makes sense to use a standard framework just to learn a little more about the client situation and then form a hypothesis five to six minutes into the case. (This often involves revising the framework to fit the hypothesis better.) But in this situation, the framework's only value is that it asks a few high-probability questions likely to uncover some information that would shape a hypothesis, based on some informed intuition.

What I am about to say is worth writing down, circling, and marking with a few stars, so remember it:

The hypothesis is more important than the framework.

It's simply *not* possible to determine the correct framework until *after* you've determined your hypothesis. (This sentence is worth rereading a few times too.)

This is *why* the case interview process is *not* a framework-driven approach but rather a hypothesis-driven one. (This is yet another point worth remembering, so mark it with some stars.)

This point is fundamental to case interviews, yet it takes some people awhile to *master*. Everyone understands it intellectually, but not everyone can master the concept to the point of *automatically* using it in an interview.

As a candidate, you want to let the *hypothesis* dictate whether you use a customized issue tree or a commonly used framework—whichever approach will best test the hypothesis is the one you want to use.

The Problem of Being "Overprepared"

One of my blog readers recently asked me, "Can a candidate be too prepared?" My short answer is yes—and no. When interviewers complain that candidates are "too prepared," they mean one of two things:

- The candidate has spent a lot of time preparing incorrectly.

- The candidate starts the case well, structures it well, and analyzes within the branches well, but he misses key insights that a candidate with this skill level does not normally miss, so the conclusion is missing certain elements.

For years, interviewers have complained about candidates being framework robots. The complaint is similar to the story about a child with a hammer who suddenly thinks that everything is a nail. Interviewers may characterize such candidates as "too prepared," but what they really mean is that the candidates prepared so incorrectly and became so entrenched in what they had memorized that they basically stopped *listening* and *thinking* logically during the case.

A case interview is a thinking game, not a memory recall game. The process of mindlessly memorizing and recalling a frame is something I call *framework vomit*. All you do is swallow a bunch of frameworks in preparation for a case interview and then vomit them all back up during the case, regardless of whether they actually work for that specific case.

Interviewers complain about the proliferation of framework vomit. They want candidates who can *think* in an interview, not just blindly recall the 15 questions associated with a particular framework. The questions aren't the key. The key is to *listen* to the answers you get to the first few of those 15 questions, *think* about what is happening (formulate a hypothesis), and then *decide* if continuing with a certain framework would be useful.

Remember, a framework is just one tool in a candidate's tool kit. If it is the *only* tool a candidate uses, then she will come across as "too prepared."

Communicate the Entire Issue Tree to an Interviewer

To communicate your issue tree clearly, you must acknowledge *all* the branches before testing the validity of the first one. Many candidates mentally construct an issue tree with three branches but initially tell the interviewer about the first branch only — after all, candidates tackle that one first. But this is a mistake. It makes it hard for the interviewer to grasp your overall problem-solving approach or structure. If the interviewer cannot see your problem-solving structure at the outset of the interview, she may conclude that you don't have one.

Interviewers want to see the *entire* problem-solving structure, not just one branch, up front to determine whether your structure is a logical test of your hypothesis. This allows the interviewer to evaluate your problem-structuring skills *before* you even begin the analysis phase.

Chapter 10

DRILL-DOWN ANALYSIS

EVERY ISSUE TREE or framework consists of components that, in aggregate, can prove or disprove your hypothesis. You need to use a process-of-elimination approach to analyze the components of your issue tree or framework.

As you work through each branch of the issue tree, you must determine if the analysis of that branch is consistent with the hypothesis. If it is, the hypothesis *might* be correct, so you should continue analyzing the remaining branches of the framework.

If analysis of a branch disproves the hypothesis, you should revise your hypothesis, reconsider what framework or issue tree is needed to test the new hypothesis, and *then* (and only then) continue your analysis. Let's look at an example:

Hypothesis: Client should enter the XYZ market.

- Consumer demand is strong, growing, and likely to stay that way.

- Client has a strong, sustainable competitive advantage in the market.

- Competition in the market is moderate and can be beaten with modest effort.

The structure of the hypothesis and the corresponding issue tree looks very similar to the structure of a logical argument. This is not an accident. Attorneys might call this type of argument a brief. In high school, my English teacher called this an expository essay. In short, it's a written argument to support a point of view.

Once you have a hypothesis and its supporting argument structure, you need to test the validity of each branch of the argument by comparing it to relevant facts, thereby testing the validity of the hypothesis overall.

Let's work through the example regarding the client entering XYZ market. The first branch that supports the hypothesis was the *guess* that "consumer demand is strong, growing, and likely to stay that way." Depending on the case interview format your interviewer uses, you will either be expected to ask the interviewer for data on the growth of consumer demand in the market or be provided a handout full of lots of data, of which only a small portion addresses growth in demand.

Let's say that once you obtain the data for this case, you determine that half the market is growing and the other half is shrinking, so it's just as likely that the data supports entering the market as it does staying out of it. As such, you cannot use this branch to validate the hypothesis.

During this phase of the case interview, it is important to say aloud what you're thinking. It's perfectly acceptable and highly encouraged for you to say, "Hmmm, if half the market is growing and the other half is shrinking, this data casts some doubt as to whether my initial hypothesis is correct."

Some candidates hesitate to say this, because they see it as an admittance that the initial hypothesis was wrong. This misplaced concern should not hold you back from thinking aloud, because the process-of-elimination approach involves eliminating conclusions that can't be true logically. Interviewers are much more concerned when the candidate's hypothesis is wrong and she doesn't realize it or do anything about it.

Interviewers cannot distinguish the candidate who doesn't recognize the logical conflict from the candidate who doesn't say *aloud* that she recognizes the logical conflict. By saying aloud what you're thinking, you ensure that the interviewer knows you recognize the logical conflict.

Let's move on to the next branch of the argument: "Client has a strong, sustainable competitive advantage in the market." It is customary for a candidate to ask questions to determine whether such a statement is true. When it comes to analyzing a client's business situation (and figuring out the right questions to ask), you'll want to understand four areas:

- Customers
- Products
- Clients
- Competition

To test the sub-hypothesis "Client has a strong, sustainable competitive advantage in the market," you need to understand the differences between the client and its competitors. For example, you could ask the following questions:

- Customers — Who are the client's customers? Where are they located? What do they want to buy? How does this information compare to competitors' customer information?
- Products — What products does the client offer versus its competitors? How do they differ?
- Client — Does the client do anything operationally that's different, unique, or unusual compared to its competitors?
- Competition — Do the competitors do anything (or choose not to do anything) operationally that's different than what the client does?

If you understand these four areas and ask appropriate questions and subsequent follow-up questions, you can determine whether it's logical to conclude that "Client has a strong, sustainable competitive advantage in the market."

If you were to determine in this branch of the analysis that the client had only a modest and temporary competitive advantage over its competitors, would it affect your initial hypothesis that the client should enter XYZ market? My initial instinct would be to revise my hypothesis to "Client should *not* enter XYZ market" because, based on the analysis of the first branch, half the market is shrinking, and the client doesn't have a long-term advantage in the market.

At this step in the case, you want to ask yourself constantly if the revised statement is true and under what circumstances it could be wrong. In the example, do you know which half of the market is growing and which half is shrinking? Once you determine this, you might rethink your earlier analysis of the client's competitive advantage and clarify the client's advantage in each market half.

If the client's main competitive advantage were in the growing part of the market, you might be more inclined to revise the initial hypothesis in a subtler way. Instead of making the hypothesis that "Client should enter the XYZ market," you clarify by saying, "Client should enter the ABC segment [the segment that's growing] of the XYZ market."

Let me explain in a bit more detail what I just said. I started off with a hypothesis and an issue tree with three components. I analyzed Component 1 (regarding market growth) and found its support for my hypothesis to be mixed. I then analyzed Component 2 of my issue tree (regarding the client's competitive advantage) and found its support for my hypothesis to be unfavorable.

What I did next was subtle—yet profoundly important: I stepped back from the branch-level analysis and *integrated* everything from the first two branches of my issue tree from a big-picture perspective. I then reconsidered the logic of my analysis to determine under what conditions my intended revisions to the hypothesis could be false.

Logically, I knew that only half the market was shrinking. This could support a variety of hypotheses, so I realized that I needed to understand that topic better before I could draw an accurate conclusion from it. Based on that one statement about the market, I could just as easily argue for the client to enter or not to enter the market. I know the client has some competitive advantage, but now that I'm *integrating* everything I've learned about the case, I wonder about the potential *interrelationship* between Branch 1 (market growth) and Branch 2 (competitive advantage): Does the client have a slight (but temporary) advantage in the shrinking portion or the growing portion of the market? This key question hasn't yet been answered.

In this example, neither branch of the analysis *alone* would indicate that one segment of the market might be a better fit than another. You must look at the big picture, taking into account everything learned from *both* branches of the issue tree, to notice a potential insight.

I attempted to revise my hypothesis to fit the newly discovered facts. I had to reconcile my hypothesis with two key facts: (1) Half the market is shrinking and the other half is growing, and (2) the client has only a modest and temporary competitive advantage.

Let's take a look at the structure (there's that word again) of the argument. Upon closer inspection, we'll find that the argument is very weak:

Hypothesis: Client should enter XYZ market.

- Fifty percent of the market is shrinking.
- Client has a modest and temporary competitive advantage.

So let's revise the statement:

Hypothesis: Client should *not* enter XYZ market.

- Fifty percent of the market is shrinking.
- Client has a modest and temporary competitive advantage.

That argument is also somewhat weak. So how can we improve it? Here's a useful comparison: In the U.S. criminal justice system, someone accused of a crime cannot be convicted unless evidence demonstrates that person's guilt "beyond a reasonable doubt." You can apply this same standard to your potential conclusions.

Do this by asking yourself if any facts support either of the two hypotheses: "Client should enter XYZ market" or "Client should *not* enter XYZ market." In this case, neither is supported particularly well.

When neither hypothesis passes the "beyond a reasonable doubt" test, two things have happened: (1) Not enough data has been obtained, and (2) the two extreme positions (enter the market versus not enter the market) have been oversimplified. The likely "right" answer is probably some nuanced option between the two extremes, and you find this answer by using a process of elimination. Video demonstrations of this process are available here: www.caseinterview.com.

Our case data so far is imperfect and incomplete, so the two extreme hypotheses seem difficult to support. At this point, it makes sense to revise both the hypothesis and the issue tree. Refining your hypothesis numerous times as you discover more information is typical of the case interview process.

Continuing with our example, we know that the two hypotheses are a stretch to support, so we need to find middle ground. Let's start with the following revisions:

Hypothesis: The client should enter one segment of the XYZ market.

- One segment of the market is growing and attractive.
- Client has at least a modest competitive advantage in this segment that can be strengthened over time.
- Competition in this segment is weak or modest.

If these three supporting statements are true, they provide reasonable support that the hypothesis is correct and thus should be considered a logical conclusion. Before we can positively conclude this, we need additional data to validate the supporting statements. The hypothesis statement and its support structure are specific and concrete, so they're very easy to test with data.

For example, in the first branch, we need to prove (or disprove) that one segment of the market is growing and attractive. Well, that's pretty easy to prove—just look at the growth rate of each segment of the market. Earlier analysis showed that half the market is growing, so we can validate this branch.

The second branch refers to the client's competitive advantage *in that segment*. To determine this, we need more information about the market segment that's growing. Is the growth driven by a certain type of customer? A certain geographical region? A certain product category? Once we know that information, we can determine the client's competitive advantage within the segment (the second branch of our issue tree) and how much competition exists within it (the third branch of our issue tree).

Let's say we discover the client doesn't have an advantage in any of the growing segments, and within these segments competition is intense. In other words, competitors have already flocked to the best parts of the market, and the client has nothing unique to add. By process of elimination, we must conclude that the client should not enter this segment or the market at all.

Through the process-of-elimination approach, you use the facts you've discovered to eliminate different hypotheses systematically. As new information becomes available through the interviewer's comments and answers to your questions, you revise the hypothesis to find the statement that comes closest to "fitting" the facts you know.

Tips for the Process-of-Elimination Process

Tip #1: Start with the Branch That Eliminates the Most Uncertainty First

Identify all the branches you intend to analyze, and then arrange them in the order in which you plan to analyze them. The first branch you analyze should reveal the most relevant, critical information—the information most likely to prove or disprove your hypothesis.

Here's an example of how to introduce your analysis during the case interview: "My hypothesis is that the client's profitability problem is driven by a revenue decline, not a cost increase. I'd like to draw out this issue tree to show both sides. I'll start with the revenue side and, if necessary, circle back to the cost side."

The second sentence shows that you have considered both branches of the framework and picked one to analyze first—the one more likely to determine whether your hypothesis is right. You need to begin your analysis this way to assure the interviewer that you intend to acknowledge the other branch(es).

As an interviewer, I automatically assume you've ignored or didn't notice the other branches if you didn't address them up front, and this is an offense that often results in a rejection.

Tip #2: Use Both Quantitative and Qualitative Analyses

A common mistake many candidates make is to stick to the type of analysis they are most comfortable with instead of taking a more balanced approach. To overgeneralize, engineers and scientists tend to err on doing only quantitative analysis. English majors tend to stick to qualitative assessments and avoid doing math.

When using a process-of-elimination approach, it's necessary to use both quantitative and qualitative analyses. The overall mix between the two types of analysis is 70/30: 70 percent quantitative and 30 percent qualitative.

To illustrate this point, let's take an example of a case that has multiple contributing factors. For our discussion, let's say we have a client that has declining profits. As you know by now, such a problem can be driven by two categories of underlying causes: a decline in revenue or an increase in cost.

A balanced candidate might listen to the background, discover there's a pricing war going on in the industry, and qualitatively conclude that the client suffers mainly from a revenue problem based on a decline in prices.

An appropriately quantitatively oriented candidate would hear that same background and seek to *quantitatively verify what she has heard qualitatively*. I can't emphasize enough the importance of this subtle distinction.

This candidate would ask for actual pricing, unit sales, and cost data going back several years. This candidate would also get comparable data for competitors. If all the competitors were facing pricing declines, then this candidate would conclude that indeed there is an industry-wide pricing problem. Otherwise, this candidate might look elsewhere. The point (and it's a key point) here is that the *balanced candidate verifies qualitative intuition with numerical data.*

Another common mistake an overly qualitative candidate will make is to fail to numerically "size" multiple potential causes of a problem. So let's assume we have another profitability case where sales have indeed declined (contributing to declines in profits) and costs have increased (also contributing to a decline in profits).

An overly qualitative candidate would be inclined to analyze changes in both sales and costs. After all, both contribute to the profit decline problem. Based on this alone, this approach is a mistake.

The balanced candidate would instead numerically measure what percentage of the total decline in profits is attributable to the decline in sales versus the increase in costs. Perhaps of the total decline in profits, 75 percent comes from a decline in sales and only 25 percent comes from an increase in costs. The balanced candidate would focus on analyzing the decline in sales first (and possibly exclusively) because it is the primary driver of the problem. Now, if such a candidate discovered that 50 percent of the profit shortfall came from a decline in sales and the other 50 percent from an increase in costs, that candidate would have no choice but to analyze both areas. The point here is that the decision of where to focus first is supported by the numerical facts, not just the qualitative intuition.

On the flip side, a candidate who's overly quantitative commonly makes a very different kind of mistake: He fails to ask for qualitative data. Typically applicants with engineering backgrounds or PhDs in quantitative fields are comfortable asking for numerical data and doing math. But many candidates from these backgrounds get stuck when they solve the math problem embedded within the case, and they have no idea what's causing the client's problem. That's because most cases involve developing both a quantitative *and* a qualitative understanding of a business.

For example, the overly quantitative candidate might determine that competitors' profit margins are 17 percent and the client's profit margin is 10 percent. This candidate might further compute that the profit problem the client faces is due entirely to a difference in how the competitors price their products versus how the client does. That said, the overly quantitative candidate can't figure out through computations alone *why* the client's prices are lower.

Quantitative analysis is very useful in answering questions regarding *what* is causing a particular symptom in a business and by *how much*. Conversely, quantitative analysis is often not useful in determining *why* a certain decision in a client organization was made and *how* certain processes (e.g., R&D, pricing decisions) in an organization are made.

Going back to my earlier example, in many cases it won't occur to the overly quantitative candidate to ask the interviewer *why* the client chose to lower prices (which in turn decreased profit margins). It's perfectly legitimate for a consultant to ask a client why something happened, and therefore it's perfectly legitimate for a candidate to ask an interviewer why something happened. For some reason, overly quantitative candidates don't realize they're "allowed" to ask a basic why question. I think they assume that the case must be solved purely with math and don't appreciate that for many cases it's simply not possible to do so.

So to recap, people who aren't quantitative enough ask too few *what* questions, such as "What percentage of the profit decline came from a drop in sales?" Those who aren't qualitative enough ask too few *how* and *why* questions, such as "Why have transportation costs gone up for the client but not for the rest of the industry?" and "How is the transportation process different for our client as compared to the rest of the industry, and why do such differences exist?"

To analyze a case well, you need to be able to ask both types of questions and to recognize when qualitative data is more useful than is quantitative, and vice versa.

Tip #3: Don't Stop Drilling Down a Branch Until You Reach a Conclusion

Over half the candidates I've worked with start analyzing a branch of an issue tree or framework but stop too soon. The other half of candidates often don't stop soon enough. The decision of when to stop going down a branch of analysis is determined 70 percent on hard data and 30 percent on judgment.

Let's start with making sure you don't stop your analysis too soon, and then we'll circle back to deciding when enough is enough and it's time to move on.

The first thing to realize about a case interview is that the majority of the time spent is *not* spent on solving the client's problem—it's spent on isolating the underlying cause of the client's problem. Most people new to case interviews routinely make this mistake.

In other words, upwards of 75 percent of the time spent on a case is on *problem definition*. And the easiest way to define the problem is to *isolate* the problem by using the process of elimination to identify what the problem is *not*.

When interviewing candidates, I've noticed that many of those who don't do well share the same bad habits. Rather than sticking to the systematic process-of-elimination approach to prove what the problem is *not*, they typically guess what the problem is:

- Maybe the client could redesign the product so it could sell better. (The candidate proposes a solution before isolating and defining the problem, basically assuming the problem is a design problem and therefore incorrectly concluding that a redesign will fix the problem.)

- Maybe the client could partner with a Fortune 500 company with more resources, and they could provide a joint offering of some type. (Again, the candidate proposes a solution without first defining and isolating the problem.)

- Maybe the client could implement a more generous sales commission program to improve sales. (The candidate assumes that product sales are causing the profit problem and that sales performance could be improved by providing higher incentives. The candidate has not proven that either assumption could be the underlying cause of the client's problem.)

Never, ever propose a solution to a case until you've isolated and defined the problem. Then and only then can you propose a solution.

If you isolate the problem exceedingly well, usually the answer is extremely obvious, so stating your recommendation is just a formality, because both you and the interviewer know the answer. If you encounter a case where the answer isn't obvious to you by the end of the case, one of three things has happened:

- You set up an incorrect issue tree.
- You didn't analyze a particular branch of the issue tree enough to eliminate it definitively as a possibility.
- The interviewer gave you a key piece of information, but you glossed over it in one branch of the issue tree, so you didn't analyze it further. Because you failed to conclude that this branch was a dead end, you wasted your time analyzing another branch — one that shouldn't have been analyzed any further.

So the trick is to drill down far enough into the branch of an issue tree to prove your hypothesis correct or incorrect, because either conclusion is useful. If your hypothesis is that your client should enter XYZ market because it's a growing market, and you discover the market is actually shrinking, then you've reached a logical conclusion on this branch of your issue tree.

Either the client *should not* enter the market due to the lack of market growth, or the client *should* enter the market due to other favorable factors that more than offset the lack of growth. You would pick either scenario as your revised hypothesis, reformulate your issue tree to test this new hypothesis, and move on to analyze a branch of this new issue tree. In either case, you're not done with this branch until you reach this decision point.

If you're certain that assessing the market's growth was a key factor in evaluating your original hypothesis, what you should *not* do is prematurely stop the analysis on growth until you can logically conclude that the market either is or is not growing.

Tip #4: When to Stop Analyzing—The Minimally Necessary Data

On the flip side, you don't want to overanalyze a branch of analysis beyond what is *minimally necessary* to test your hypothesis. To grasp this concept, we refer to the 80/20 rule, which states that 80 percent of the results come from 20 percent of the potential causes. As it applies to case interview problem solving, it means that you want to find the "minimally necessary" data to test your hypothesis.

In applying this to our prior example, if we know the market isn't growing but is actually shrinking, we can very quickly conclude that market growth alone does *not* support the hypothesis that the client should enter the market. This represents a minimally necessary amount of data to reach this conclusion.

What we do *not* need to analyze is whether the market is shrinking at 5 percent per year or 20 percent per year. This level of detail exceeds the minimally necessary level of data to reach the conclusion.

Anytime you analyze a situation beyond what is minimally necessary, the interviewer considers that highly inefficient and counts it against you during the case interview.

Tip #5: Use Diagrams (Not Just Text Blurbs) to Take Notes

I've been extremely surprised by how poorly many candidates—including people who ended up getting offers at McKinsey, Bain, and the other top firms—take notes during my mock interviews. In a 40-minute case interview, I've seen candidates take eight pages of notes! Candidates can't possibly remember what they were thinking when they wrote down notes seven pages earlier.

I encourage taking notes, but I discourage taking notes in a list format. If you take notes in a very specific way, you'll avoid getting confused by what you wrote down earlier in the interview.

I recommend taking notes on two different sets of paper. The first set focuses on the structure of the case and should be kept very neat. It should consist exclusively of issue tree diagrams and your hypotheses. Even if you're interrupted ten times during your interview, you won't have to worry about where you are in your notes. Your hypotheses and issue trees will be neatly organized in your first set of papers, so both you and the interviewer need only look at the papers to determine where you are in the structure of the case.

The second set of papers is solely for you to do computations; think of it as a scratch pad. Use this set to determine whether a particular part of the issue can be eliminated mathematically as a possible cause of the problem at hand.

Once you answer the question for that branch of the case, you don't have to refer back to the scratch pad anymore. You've reached your intermediate conclusion, so make the appropriate notation on the issue tree diagram.

It doesn't matter if your calculation notes take up six or seven pages, because the important information, such as your *conclusions* and *structure*, is in a single, easy-to-reference place.

When you determine a branch isn't relevant to the key issue at hand, I recommend putting an X near that branch to remind you—and the interviewer—that you've eliminated that branch. Deliberately show the interviewer that you've eliminated that branch and have three branches left.

Repeat this process with each branch so the interviewer can see which logical branches are left. Because the interviewer doesn't know exactly what you're thinking, you want her to *see* this process of elimination on paper. At the end of this process, one branch remains: the root cause of the client's problems.

Why the Process of Elimination Works

Clients commonly misunderstand their own problems. They sometimes incorrectly assume that a visible result they do not like, such as a decline in sales or profits, is the problem, not realizing that the visible issue is just a symptom of the underlying problem.

But you can't tell clients flat out they're wrong; they'll resist and not believe you. It's akin to you telling an interviewer, before you've done any analysis, that the answer to a case involving a profitability problem is to fix pricing. Absent justification, the interviewer wouldn't have any confidence in your answer, even if it were right.

This is why strong analytical, not intuitive, problem-solving abilities are so highly desired in consultants. Both types of abilities are equally valuable in running a business, but only the analytical problem solver is adept at advising an executive.

Clients probably have a lot of intuitive problem solvers on staff already, and each employee has his or her own opinion. But clients need someone to use facts to determine which of those opinions are the best. Not only that, they need everyone on the client team to agree on the solution. Recommending a solution to a client is completely different than having the entire client team agree on it.

If you involve all the client team members (or interviewers) in your approach—and thereby your process of elimination— they'll see you systematically tackle each branch of an issue tree and cross out certain branches as you eliminate them. In doing this, you not only show the clients your process but also involve them in it directly. If you demonstrated to the client why you've eliminated X and Y as the problem, then by the time you get to Z the client has no choice but to accept the final conclusion, even if it's one the client dislikes.

I recently took a client through this process, and one of the team members said to me, "It was very interesting that you did not just tell us the answer, but rather you led us to the answer." I did so deliberately. People support what they help build, so if you involve all client team members in the process, they're more likely to support the conclusion.

Similarly, if you involve the interviewer in your process, he is more likely to support your conclusion. The interviewer will also note how easy (or difficult) it is to follow your process and how much you've included him in the process.

Now that we've covered the process-of-elimination approach, let's transition to closing out a case interview with a strong synthesis.

Chapter 11

SYNTHESIS

SYNTHESIS, IN SIMPLE terms, is a way to summarize progress made during a case interview. You use it at the end of a case interview to tell the interviewer what you've learned.

In addition, I strongly recommend you synthesize any progress you make throughout the case, especially anytime you switch to a new branch in your issue tree or revise your hypothesis. Unlike a standard summary, which usually involves recapping what's transpired throughout the case, a synthesis follows a specific communication structure:

State action-oriented recommendation/conclusion

- Supporting point 1
- Supporting point 2
- Supporting point 3

Restate recommendation/conclusion

This top-down communication structure is the de facto standard for communicating with senior executives in consulting and in industry—and for communicating in a case interview. Most people tend to use a bottom-up summary approach intuitively, but this approach is not well-suited for the case interview.

To help you understand the differences between these two approaches, let me provide a nonbusiness example. Imagine you ask a friend, "How was your vacation?" Here's what a bottom-up answer might look like:

- First, airport security was a mess, and they treated me like a criminal.
- Then our first flight was delayed three hours.
- We missed our connecting flight.

- Because our flights were late, the cruise ship left without us.
- We caught a flight on a small plane to the cruise ship's second port of call.
- Our room wasn't prepared.
- While waiting for our room, I slipped, fell, and broke my leg.
- I wasn't able to swim in the pool.
- I wasn't able to play on the beach.
- I wasn't able to go shopping.
- My medical bills cost $3,000, which I wasn't expecting before we went on the trip.

This is a bottom-up summary—not synthesis—so it's marked by lots of details and activities. It lacks a clear one-sentence conclusion, concise and organized supporting evidence (three pieces of supporting evidence, ideally), and a restatement of the one-sentence conclusion. Here's what a top-down synthesis of your friend's vacation might look like:

My vacation was lousy for three reasons:

- I missed the plane and thus the cruise ship.
- I broke my leg and was confined to a wheelchair.
- I paid $3,000 in medical bills for the privilege of watching others have fun.

Those are the three reasons why my vacation was lousy.

You'll notice several differences between the bottom-up summary and the top-down synthesis. First, the synthesis is much shorter. Second, if you have time to hear the first sentence only, you understand the *essential message* in only four words: "My vacation was lousy." You might not get details until the second, third, or fourth sentence, but this efficient form of communication gets to the main idea very quickly.

Third, the message has a clear beginning, middle, and end, and together the beginning and the end emphasize the *essential message* not once but twice. The conclusion, which actually appears first, has a clear supporting rationale. If the reasons supporting the conclusion make sense, it's fairly easy to accept and ultimately agree with the conclusion.

Interviewers highly value this synthesis communication format because senior executive clients (CEOs, CFOs, COOs, etc.) value it. Senior executives are extremely busy running a business that makes $500 million to $1+ billion yearly. If a business generates, say, $1 billion every year, that's approximately $3 million in revenue every *day*, a little over $100,000 in revenue every *hour*, and around $1,500 in revenue every minute. If you take 30 minutes to explain something that could have been explained in five minutes to a senior executive client, you've wasted 30 minutes of the client's time—and more than $50,000 of the company's money.

This example may not be mathematically true or perfect, but it conveys senior executives' thoughts when forced to sit through bottom-up presentations that could have been replaced by concise, much shorter top-down presentations. When you waste senior executive clients' time, they think about all the other things they could've and should've been doing instead. You don't want to be known for wasting anyone's time. In fact, your manager and partner won't allow you to do it, which is why interviewers pay such close attention to your ability to synthesize effectively.

Two things surprise members of my website (www.caseinterview.com) who have received multiple job offers: (1) my endless emphasis on this type of communication, and (2) interviewers' responses to candidates who follow my advice.

I constantly emphasize and reemphasize just how important this type of communication is. I even suggest that candidates audio-record themselves communicating their synthesis, play it back, and analyze it. If even one word is off, rerecord the whole thing. Candidates who do this over and over and over again ultimately master this communication skill.

This sounds like overkill, but when I look back on my first two years at McKinsey, a solid 80 percent of my managers' feedback related to communication skills. They rarely gave me any feedback on my math skills, quantitative analysis skills, spreadsheets, or models. Once you are working as a consultant, everyone emphasizes the development of this skill. If you can demonstrate mastery of this communication skill during the recruiting process, you will set yourself apart from most other candidates.

The other thing that surprises members of my website who have gotten multiple job offers is how favorably interviewers respond to candidates who have followed my advice. Successful candidates tell me that once they receive job offers, the interviewers go to great effort to compliment them on their communication skills.

So when you're competing against candidates who are all strong analytically, the best communicator often wins. Given the choice between a first-year consultant who's good with spreadsheets and a first-year consultant who's good with spreadsheets *and* could communicate effectively with a senior client, firms always go with the latter.

Examples of Synthesis

I recently exchanged emails with a case interview beginner who'd passed McKinsey's first-round interview but was told synthesis was her weak spot. McKinsey suggested she work on improving that skill before her second-round interview. She asked me to help her better understand why her synthesis was weak.

In the first-round interview, the interviewer asked the candidate whether a nonprofit client should expand Program B in the short term. (Note: The actual case isn't relevant. Just pay attention to the structure of the communication.) Here's how this candidate synthesized her findings at the end of the case, in her own words:

> I recommended that the client expand Program B for the following reasons:
>
> - Currently, Program A is losing money and cannot sustain itself.

- *Program B is highly profitable.*

If we can expand the program by just X percent, it can help the client break even. However, there is concern among the employees that expanding Program B is against the mission statement of helping Program A members. We should address it by doing the following:

- *Educate the employees that Program B does not go against the mission statement but rather enhances Program A by providing the funding and bringing the program to a broader public.*

- *Encourage employees to enroll in Program B and learn from the interaction with Program B members that the program brings impact to both Program A and Program B.*

In summary, we should expand Program B in the short term.

Before I point out what was wrong with this particular synthesis attempt, see if you notice the problems. OK, here's what I noticed:

- There were too many points.

- Not all the points supported the main conclusion, and some were sub-points of the point that supported the main conclusion. Sound confusing? That's because it *is* confusing.

- The candidate clearly recommended expanding Program B, but based on what I read I'd be hard-pressed to explain in a sentence or two *why* that was the right decision.

As I mentioned, the ideal structure for a strong synthesis is the following:

State action-oriented recommendation/conclusion

- Supporting point 1
- Supporting point 2
- Supporting point 3

Restate recommendation/conclusion

Keep in mind:

- You can state up to three reasons—never more.
- The conclusion is always first—always.

I suggested to this candidate that she use my feedback to revise the closing from her McKinsey interview. Here's her second attempt, in her own words:

> Based on the initial analysis, I recommend that the company expand Program B in the short term for the following reasons:
>
> - Currently, Program A is losing money and cannot sustain itself.
> - Program B is highly profitable. If we can expand the program by just X percent, the company can break even quickly.
> - There are risks involved in expanding Program B, in particular the reputation risk. But due to the short-term nature of the expansion, these risks can be minimized.
>
> Given more time, we should evaluate options to turn around Program A and to unwind Program B.

I told her I wasn't sure what she meant by "unwind," and because I didn't know the actual case, I couldn't tell if I agreed with that portion of her conclusion. Aside from that word, the rest of her synthesis was good. The conclusion was clear. *Three* easy-to-understand reasons supported her conclusion.

If I were to nitpick (which I've been known to do), I would say her last sentence should have restated the conclusion by saying, "And that's why I recommend the client expand Program B in the short term."

Instead of saying only "Given more time, we should evaluate options to turn around Program A and to unwind Program B," it would have been better to say, "That's why I recommend that the client expand Program B in the short term.

In addition, given more time, we should evaluate options to turn around Program A and to unwind Program B."

You will notice that in my restatement of the candidate's conclusion, I included the rephrasing that starts with "Given more time ..." In this example, the candidate used an advanced strategy in her conclusion—she stated the additional analysis she'd be inclined to do if she had more time. Quite often the case interview ends because you've run out of time, not because you've completed every possible analysis for the case. If that happens, incorporate wording into the standard synthesis structure to explain what remaining uncertainties you have and what you'd analyze next if given additional time.

Partners sell "phase 2" of an engagement by indicating what additional certainty the consulting team could've discovered if it'd had more time. Partners also use this structure with clients during interim progress review presentations, such as the presentation at the end of the second month in a six-month project.

This structure synthesizes what you know, indicates what else you need to know, and lays out your plan to address those remaining issues. Use this approach anytime you think you've run out of time or when you have a pretty clear idea what your conclusion is but don't have time to address one or two areas. Feeling like you're short on time is common, and by no means should you think of it as failing the interview.

Returning to our example synthesis, I contacted the candidate after reading her revised synthesis and asked if she thought it more accurately reflected her thinking than did the first version. She wrote back:

> *The new version still reflects my original thinking but is more to the point. If I were the client, I would like the new version too.*
>
> *To be honest, I am still a little unsure about the third point—risks can be minimized. During the interview, I solved the profit problem and identified the benefits and risks quickly, but I spent all the remaining time (about half of the interview time) exploring ideas of how to manage one particular risk—reputation risk.*

The objective of the case was to determine whether or not to expand Program B; I didn't understand the intention of this in-depth "idea generating" question.

Because we spent so much time on it, I thought it deserved a mention in the synthesis. Obviously I was wrong; the synthesis should be conclusion-driven and focus on the big picture. I'll practice more for the next round.

I told the candidate I thought her second attempt was much better too. I recommended that she note any remaining issues— and in actual client work, there always are some—following her conclusion. I said:

Nothing you said in your synthesis supported your point on unwinding Program B. You need to say, "After the short-term crisis has passed, it would be worth examining if Program B — the temporary solution — should be canceled ..." or something like that.

A point like that is most appropriate to mention as an add-on to the primary conclusion and three key supporting points, not to replace that structure.

I used it all the time in client presentations and conversations at McKinsey, especially in the middle of a client engagement where we had some early conclusions but still had more things left to analyze.

The way you synthesized the case the second time was clean and well-done. Repeat the process in future interviews and you will do well on that aspect of the case.

When to Synthesize

You should synthesize the case not only at the end of the interview but also *throughout* the case. Most candidates don't use this advanced technique. It's certainly possible to get a job offer without synthesizing throughout the case, but it's far easier to stand out when you do.

When you synthesize during the case, the format is more abbreviated and flexible. The conclusion still is first, but sometimes you have only one or two supporting points.

Here's a quick example: You're asked to work with a client that had a $10 million profit decline last year. The client wants to find a way to fix that situation. You analyze sales (remember, profit = sales - costs) and determine that they remain unchanged from the prior year. We know via math that if profit has declined by $10 million and sales have remained unchanged, then costs must have gone up by $10 million. There are two ways to handle this:

- Say, "Now that I've analyzed sales, I'd like to analyze costs next."
- Say, "I can conclude that sales are not causing the profit problem, because first, sales have remained unchanged in the past year, and second, costs have gone up by $10 million and account for 100 percent of the problem. I would like to analyze costs now to understand better which costs have increased and why."

The synthesis in the second version is *much* better. In those two sentences, you remind the interviewer of the overall problem-solving structure (that you finished the sales branch and now need to move on to the cost branch of the issue tree), you firmly conclude what the problem is *not* (reflecting the process-of-elimination analytical approach that firms value so much), you lead with a conclusion, and you support the conclusion.

In general, you want to use this type of mini-synthesis anytime you switch branches in your issue tree or revise your hypothesis (usually in response to having discovered some quantitative or qualitative insight about the case).

To watch video demonstrations of how to synthesize properly, see the video tutorials available on my website at www.caseinterview.com.

PART FOUR

Frameworks

Chapter 12

CORE FRAMEWORKS

The Role of Frameworks

As mentioned elsewhere in this book, a framework is an issue tree template used to solve a common business problem. Before I introduce you to the three main frameworks I used when I was a candidate, it's important to note that there is no official list of frameworks in the industry. Frameworks are simply a way to structure your analysis. Consulting firms often have a set of frameworks they use for client work, and individual consultants have their own set of frameworks. The list I'll share with you comprises *my* personal set of frameworks.

I didn't invent my frameworks; I saw other candidates in the recruiting process use similar ones, and I tweaked those frameworks so that they made sense to me. It's the personalization that makes these frameworks mine.

I suggest that you start to learn my frameworks by memorizing them exactly as I lay them out here. Eventually, you'll want to customize the frameworks to fit the peculiarities of each specific case you're dealing with. In other words, before you learn how to break the "rules," you first need to master them.

In addition, I can't emphasize enough how critical it is for you to realize that a framework is really just an issue tree, and an issue tree is designed to test your hypothesis. The objective of a case interview is *not* to memorize and then use a framework. The objective *is* to test the hypothesis. *I cannot emphasize this enough:* If you memorize and recall frameworks during an interview but never actually test the hypothesis, *you will get rejected.*

The Core Frameworks

The frameworks I used most often as a candidate were the following:

- Profitability
- Business situation
- Mergers and acquisitions

These three frameworks, or portions of them, cover approximately 70 percent of the cases you'll likely receive. The profitability framework is used in about 25 percent of cases, the business situation framework in roughly 50 percent of cases, and the mergers and acquisitions framework (which is derived from the business situation framework) in about 10 percent of cases. The total of 85 percent doesn't match the 70 percent figure above because some cases involve multiple frameworks.

If you master the first two frameworks—profitability and business situation—and use the custom issue tree process described previously, you should be well-prepared for more than 98 percent of all cases you're likely to receive.

In addition, if only a portion of a framework is necessary to test your hypothesis, use only that portion. Do *not* use the entire framework. (Interviewers complain that weak candidates often use an entire framework even though in a particular case only one-quarter of the framework is relevant.)

Remember, using the framework *is not* the goal. Testing the hypothesis *is*.

The Case Against Memorizing Too Many Frameworks

I completely disagree with the school of thought in the case interview preparation community that endorses memorizing 12 or more frameworks rather than the core three that I suggest. The rationale for that approach is that interviewers present many different types of cases, so the more frameworks candidates know, the better prepared they are. On paper, this makes a lot of sense, but in practice the approach is flawed for three reasons:

- Insufficient time to learn so many frameworks
- Lack of mastery of any framework

- Over-reliance on memorizing more frameworks at the expense of mastering how to formulate a hypothesis and a custom issue tree to test the hypothesis

If you memorize 12 or more frameworks, you'll be able to cover about 80 percent of cases. If you memorize my three frameworks, you'll be able to cover about 70 percent of cases. Is it worth memorizing three times as many frameworks to cover only 10 percent more cases? I don't think so, because you hit the point of diminishing returns very quickly.

Candidates who try to memorize and get really good at using at least 12 frameworks usually have about 40 percent proficiency in all those frameworks. I think that being 100 percent proficient in two or three frameworks is a much better bet, especially considering you can develop your issue tree skills to handle anything the frameworks don't address. It's impossible to memorize enough frameworks to cover every case interview scenario, so even if you memorize 100 frameworks, you can't guarantee you'll be prepared for 100 percent of the cases you might face.

Working consultants face the same challenge. When I worked at McKinsey, I rarely used a standard framework in my client work. Instead, I used a custom issue tree pretty much every single day. There's an important lesson here worth noting.

When to Use Each Type of Framework

With the foregoing lesson in mind, let's focus on when to use each type of framework and then delve into the details of each.

The Profitability Framework

The profitability framework is useful for isolating the mathematical cause of a drop in profit, so it may be applicable when it's unclear why a client is losing money. It's an excellent tool for developing a *quantitative* understanding of the client's business, not for determining why these quantitative changes are happening.

For example, using the profitability framework, you might be able to determine that a client's profits have declined due to an industry-wide price war. But the framework can't explain *why* the price war is happening and why it is happening now. To understand the latter, you need to develop a qualitative understanding of the client's business.

The Business Situation Framework

The business situation framework is useful for developing a conceptual and qualitative understanding of a client's business, market, and industry. Each component of the framework lists certain questions that you might want to consider asking or learning more about. We'll get to those questions later.

Applying this framework to the example above, you discover that a new competitor with advanced technology and an efficient cost structure has entered the market, which likely caused the price war.

The strength of this framework is that it helps uncover conceptual information that provides insight into what's going on in the case. The weakness of this framework is that it's not quantitative enough on its own.

For example, using only standard framework questions, you might discover the presence of a new competitor with a lower cost structure. This is a critical insight because you now know *why* the industry is experiencing a price war.

The business situation framework does not, however, prompt you to ask, "*How much* lower is the competitor's cost structure than everyone else's?" That question is one that would come to you based on your qualitative discovery (the existence of the new competitor) and subsequent translation of it into quantitative terms.

In a case interview, you want to constantly bounce back and forth between quantitative and qualitative analysis. You need to use *both* types of analysis to succeed.

I notice that candidates with PhDs in math and the sciences love the quantitative (mathematical) aspects of the profitability framework but are relatively uncomfortable with the business situation framework, which they find fuzzy, imprecise, and qualitative.

Many of these candidates hope their case interview will be one big math problem. When they do all the math that's possible to do in a case and then realize they still have no idea what's going on in the client's business, they finally understand that you can't use math alone to pass a case interview. You must do qualitative analysis too.

Conversely, candidates from liberal arts and creative backgrounds seem to like the business situation framework because it considers many of the commonsense aspects of a business. Yet these candidates struggle to convert qualitative insight into quantitative measurement and tend to focus on interesting but not always mathematically relevant issues.

The Mergers and Acquisitions Framework

You might use the mergers and acquisitions framework to address cases in which one company wants to acquire or merge with another company. It is best used to determine the conceptual "fit" between two companies: Does joining these two companies have a multiplicative effect, where the whole is more valuable than the sum of its parts? Because this framework is really just a twist on the business situation framework, it too is qualitative in nature and similarly does not quantitatively measure the impact of the qualitative discoveries.

Applying this framework to our example, you might discover that the big company has a huge sales force and many customers but not enough products to sell. You might also discover that the little company has a small sales force and really valuable products that the big company's customers really want. The mergers and acquisitions framework doesn't prompt you to quantify the increase in sales that would result from having the big company's sales force sell the little company's product. That requires math, and although such a mathematical estimate would be useful, calculating that number is not part of the framework.

In addition, the two companies could be worth more combined than as separate entities, but the framework doesn't address the cost side of an acquisition. Sure, the combined company would grow sales faster, but how much would the acquiring company have to pay to get the deal? Would there be a good return on investment?

This is where combining frameworks with custom issue trees can come in handy. In our example, we could combine the mergers and acquisitions framework with a variation of the profitability framework to measure whether the benefits from the acquisition would outweigh the costs.

Chapter 13

PROFITABILITY FRAMEWORK

THE PROFITABILITY FRAMEWORK helps you take a company's financial profits and mathematically deconstruct them into component parts.

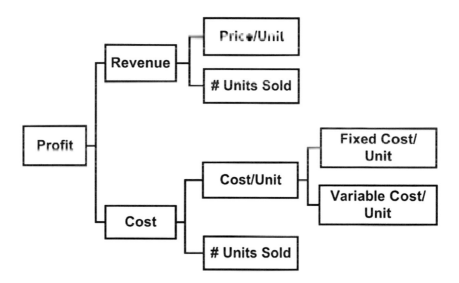

Figure 4: Profitability Framework

Printable Version: A PDF of this framework diagram is available for free at www.caseinterview.com/bonus.

Profits comprise two branches in this issue tree: revenues and cost. Here's the profit formula once again:

Profits = revenues - costs

Revenues and costs have sub-component branches. Let's review one branch and sub-branch at a time to answer common questions about them and to learn what you should be doing as you go through the analysis.

If you have a profit problem, you need to figure out if it's revenue- or cost-driven. If it's revenue-driven, look at units sold versus revenue per unit, so

Revenue = unit price x number of units sold

If the interviewer is kind, the problem will be only revenue-driven or only cost-driven. If he is unkind, you might be told that units shipped have dropped *and* prices have dropped, meaning that two factors have made profits worse.

Once you've reached this level, you have a lot of work ahead of you. Most cases are very mechanical, systematic, and situation-dependent. What you do next depends entirely on what information you just uncovered.

Segmenting and Isolating

When you work down a branch of an issue tree such as the profitability framework, remember to isolate and segment. For example, let's say you've *segmented* (broken up into component pieces) profits into sales and costs and determined that a decline in sales is driving the bulk of the decline in profits. By making this determination, you've *isolated* the problem via the process of elimination. It's actually only a decline in sales, not a cost problem. This process of segmenting and isolating worked, so now you repeat it.

Next, segment units sold into its component parts. Determine which components of units sold have caused most of the problem. At that point, say to the interviewer, "I'd like to segment units sold into its component parts. Do we have any information on the components that drive units sold?" Let's say the interviewer says, "Yes, in Europe, units sold are up 20 percent, and in Asia they're down 20 percent."

The reason you say to the interviewer "I'd like to segment this metric into its component parts" instead of "I'd like to segment units sold by geography" is because there are often multiple ways you could segment. For example, you could have just as easily segmented units sold by product line, reseller type, customer type, or price point. The options here are truly infinite.

If in the background of the case the interviewer *deliberately* gave you information that would suggest a particular segmentation pattern, then use that information to segment your numbers. If there isn't any obvious segmentation pattern, avoid stating the segmentation pattern you want to see. Instead, phrase your question such that the interviewer tells you which segmentation pattern is the right one to use.

Because there are lots of ways to segment, don't waste time trying to figure out what the interviewer is looking for. Just tell the interviewer you want to segment and open the door for him to tell you which way you ought to segment, because usually the interviewer will have one preferred way.

In general, you score points in the interview for recognizing the need to segment, not for guessing the right segmentation pattern. (In practice, most consultants will try up to 20 segmentation patterns and discover the most insightful one only through trial and error.)

Now that you've segmented, it's time to isolate the problem by noticing in which parts of the business the problem does and does not exist. As you "drill down," you ignore the parts of the business where the problem does not exist to focus on the areas where it does. Once you've isolated the root cause, say, "This profitability problem is actually being driven by a decline in sales volume in China" (and not anywhere else).

You will do one of two things as soon as you've exhausted what you can determine mathematically in the case: (1) Refine your hypothesis and create a custom issue tree to drive the rest of your analysis, or (2) shift to understand qualitatively what you've determined quantitatively as the root cause of the client's problem.

Going back to our earlier example, you've used segmentation, isolation, and the process of elimination to determine that sales volume in China has dropped severely, but you still don't know *why*. At this point, it makes sense to switch to the business situation framework to understand qualitatively *why* sales volume in China has dropped so severely.

Drilling Down and Pulling Up

Interviewers often use the phrase *drilling down* (into the branches of an issue tree) to describe the process-of-elimination approach you should use.

For example, in the opening of a profitability case, you segment profits into its two component parts—sales and costs. Let's say that half of the decline in profits comes from a decline in sales, and the other half comes from an increase in costs. Based on this information, both branches of the issue tree are relevant, so you can't eliminate either one. So you need to drill down one of the branches until you've segmented and isolated several times to figure out what's causing the problem. Then you need to pull up to the top of the issue tree and drill down the other branch.

Let's say you drilled down the cost branch and determined that a rise in labor costs caused overall costs to increase. Assuming you cannot proceed any further because there's no logical next step, you need to pull up to the two components of profits: revenues and costs. Because you already drilled down the cost branch, you need to drill down the revenue branch.

Sample Analysis

The following example shows you the steps you might take in drilling down the cost branch of an issue tree.

Disaggregating Costs

You need to break down (segment and isolate) cost into its component parts, and you can do this in many different ways. When there's no obvious reason to do this a particular way, by default I break down costs into units sold and cost per unit. I use this breakdown because later in the analysis process it allows me to analyze easily the *profit per unit*, which is useful for a number of reasons. If the profit per unit has remained steady but the number of units sold has fallen, then as revenues decline, so do costs:

Revenues = fewer # units x same price

Costs = fewer # units x same cost per unit

This math shows logically that the underlying problem is the decline in the number of units sold.

Without knowing the profit per unit, you can easily get distracted by the fact that costs have declined alongside profits. (Normally, when profits decline, costs increase, not decrease.) This can be very confusing, but by disaggregating sales into price per unit and costs into cost per unit, you can determine the underlying cause of the profit decline.

Distinguishing Fixed vs. Variable Costs

Next, I like to break down cost per unit into fixed costs and variable costs. It's extremely important that you truly understand the concept of *fixed* versus *variable* costs. Most candidates understand these terms generally, but few grasp the actual concept.

A *fixed cost* doesn't change as the number of units sold changes.

Let's say you pay $5 million a year in rent for the company's headquarters building. It doesn't matter whether you sell 1 unit or 1 million units, because your rent is set at $5 million yearly.

A *variable cost* changes, typically linearly, with the number of units sold. For example, materials costs and sales force commission expenses grow and shrink *proportionally* as the number of units sold increases or decreases.

The differences between fixed and variable costs are *profoundly* important to running a profitable business. The following example demonstrates why.

Assume two companies are unprofitable and losing equal amounts of profit each year. Company 1 has high fixed costs but very low variable costs. In other words, the company's profit per unit is very high. This business is unprofitable because the number of units sold is too low relative to the magnitude of fixed costs. Company 2 has low fixed costs but extremely high variable costs. The company's per-unit variable costs are actually higher than the price per unit—it costs the company $3 to manufacture a product it sells for $2.

On the surface, the companies have identical problems, but their root causes couldn't be more different.

Company 1 must grow the number of units sold. With sufficient volume, the profitability problem will fix itself. In other words, this company can grow its way out of its profitability problem.

If Company 2 doubles the number of units sold, it loses twice as much money and will go out of business twice as quickly. In this company's case, you need to answer two fundamental questions:

- Is there any way to charge a price higher than per-unit variable costs?

- Is there any way to dramatically reduce per-unit variable costs?

The consultant's (and the case interview candidate's) role is to dig beneath the symptoms of the client's problems to find the root cause of those problems. Clients know that understanding these insights can be quite useful and can lead to counterintuitive but factually correct decisions.

With regard to Company 2, perhaps the VP of sales wants his sales force to sell more and thereby increase the number of units sold. To temporarily solve the profitability problem, however, it would make more sense for the sales force to *shrink* the number of units sold. This won't fix the problem in the long run, but it will help the company lose money more slowly.

Segmenting Costs

When analyzing costs, it's often useful to segment them into fixed versus variable costs. You can do this in two ways.

One way is to disaggregate your cost per unit into fixed costs per unit and variable costs per unit. Remember that fixed costs per unit is an allocated figure, so if the number of units sold increases, the portion of fixed costs "allocated" to each unit declines. As such, fixed costs per unit is a moving target, whereas variable costs per unit tends to be more stable. So the structure in this case would be:

Costs

- Number of units sold
- Cost per unit
  - o Variable cost per unit
  - o Fixed cost per unit

The other way is to segment by aggregated fixed costs and aggregated variable costs first and then segment variable costs into number of units sold and variable cost per unit:

Costs

- Fixed costs
- Variable costs
  - o Number of units sold
  - o Variable cost per unit

What segmentation method should you use? Tell your interviewer you want to segment costs, and see what she says. The interviewer will usually give you the data in a way that implies a preferred segmentation pattern.

Expecting the Unexpected

To complicate a case—and make it more realistic—costs can be further segmented by cost category, such as labor, raw materials, shipping, and rent.

When you tell the interviewer you want to segment, she might not want you to segment by either of the two patterns above. Instead, the interviewer might give you costs by spending category, which is how most clients track costs on their financial statements. If this happens, segment and isolate based on the segmentation pattern the interviewer gives you.

Another way to segment is by steps in a process. Perhaps a manufacturing process has three steps to it. In response to your desire to segment costs, the interviewer might tell you the costs for each step of the process:

- Step 1: $100,000
- Step 2: $300,000
- Step 3: $250,000

I point out these variations (of which there are really an infinite number) to remind you to be *flexible* in your thinking. It's always correct to segment costs and isolate the primary driver for a profitability problem driven by increased costs, but *how* you segment will vary from case to case. These frameworks are intended to be used *flexibly*. Don't ever forget that.

Always, Always, Always Compare Your Metrics to Something Else

As you segment your numbers, use the process of elimination to isolate the primary driver of a profit problem. At some point in the process, you'll discover a number you don't know how to interpret.

For example, let's say your interviewer tells you a client's variable cost per unit is $5,000. Is that good or bad? High or low? The absolute number is pretty useless unless you compare it to something else. In my experience, the two most useful comparisons to make are the following:

- Compare a metric to itself in a previous time period.
- Compare a metric to the rest of the industry.

Depending on the comparison you make, $5,000 in per-unit variable costs could be good or bad, high or low. If I told you per-unit variable costs were $4,000 last year, you'd conclude that the per-unit variable costs had increased dramatically, and a story would begin to unfold.

A different story would unfold if I told you a competitor's per-unit variable costs were $4,000 last year and remained constant this year. Why did the client's per-unit variable costs go up $1,000 but the competitor's didn't change at all?

The preliminary conclusion here is that the profitability problem the client faces is a company-specific problem, not an industry-wide problem. Determining the root cause is important, because having to reframe it later could fundamentally shift your hypothesis and the subsequent issue tree or framework you use to test it.

For example, if the problem is clearly a company-specific problem, it doesn't make sense to analyze competitors. It makes sense to analyze the client's operations and perhaps circle back to competitors later if something you discover about the client's operations warrants a comparison to competitors.

Just as with the business situation framework, which is the focus of the next chapter, knowing where to focus helps direct the rest of your problem-solving efforts.

Chapter 14

BUSINESS SITUATION FRAMEWORK

THE BUSINESS SITUATION framework is appropriate for a wide variety of client and company situations, including introducing a new market entry or a new product, starting a new business, opening a lemonade stand, developing a growth strategy, divesting, or making a turnaround. This framework will help you understand what qualitative issues drive and impact a business overall.

The framework consists of four key components. I draw this framework as four distinct boxes, but you could quite easily redraw it as an issue tree with four branches:

- Customer
- Product
- Company
- Competition

The business situation framework demonstrates that when making all different types of business decisions, it's useful to consider data related to customers, the product or products involved, the company (typically your client), and competition.

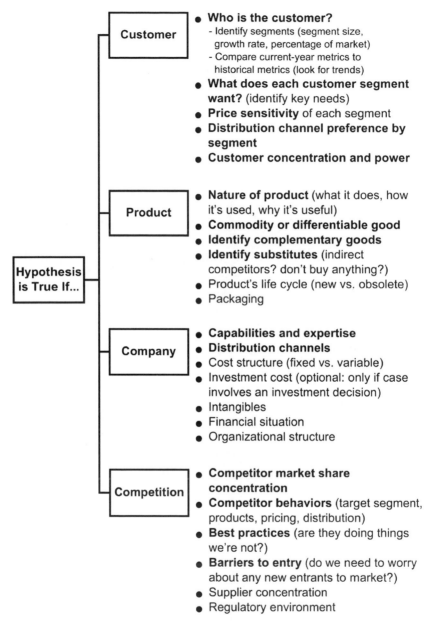

Figure 5: Business Situation Framework

Note: Bolded items are relevant in a higher percentage of cases.

Printable Version: A PDF of this diagram is available for free at www.caseinterview.com/bonus.

Each of the four branches has its own list of questions to ask or learn more about. It may be tempting to work through the framework diagram mentally and ask all the questions it lists. But by now, you know this is a big mistake. You need to let your hypothesis guide your decision about which of the questions in the diagram—and others not in the diagram—are *relevant* in testing the hypothesis.

If you start a case with absolutely no background information, this framework is used *initially* as an information-gathering tool. The questions in the diagram are what I call *high-probability questions*. When answered, these questions give you a very high probability of discovering some insight about the case—*enough insight to prompt you to refine your hypothesis.*

Once you have enough insight to state a refined hypothesis, you'll want to do one of two things: (1) Work through the rest of the framework, *excluding* questions that aren't necessary to test your hypothesis; or (2) develop your own custom issue tree and questions that will better test your refined hypothesis.

For example, let's say that during your analysis you discover something indicating that the client's key issue is internal, not related to its competitors. Instead of answering all the questions in the competitor section of the framework, revise your hypothesis to say that the client's key issue is internal, and switch to the company portion of the framework (or in some cases, create a custom issue tree).

Stated differently, frameworks are yours to play with. You can use a whole framework, one of its major components, or just a subset of the questions in one of the components. Frameworks are *flexible*.

The business situation framework helps you uncover insightful information that will allow you to create a better-informed hypothesis, so once you've revised your hypothesis, let it determine whether you continue with the framework, continue with parts of the framework selectively, or drop the framework entirely and use a custom issue tree instead.

Customer Analysis

Let's go through the mechanical stuff and look at the kind of questions I typically ask, starting with analysis of the customer portion of the framework. The following questions help you qualitatively analyze customers in a market. When a case requires understanding customers better, I will often use a subset of these questions to kick off my customer analysis.

It is important to note that depending on the answers to my first few questions, I will dynamically change which of the remaining questions I choose to ask. In addition, I'll decide which questions to ask that are not on the list but come to mind as being relevant based on the answers to my initial questions.

Below are some of these initial questions:

- Who is the customer?
- What are the customer's segment needs?
- What is each segment's price sensitivity?
- What are each segment's distribution channel preferences?
- What is the customer concentration in each segment?

Who Is the Customer?

In kicking off a customer analysis, it's useful to ask a very basic question: "Who is the customer?"

Sometimes there's more than one type of customer, so you need to identify not only the customer but also the key customer segments. Once you know this information, you need to quantify it. If there are three customer segments, how big is each segment? Which ones are growing or shrinking?

Once you have both a qualitative and a quantitative understanding of the various customer segments, move on to the next analysis.

What Are the Customer's Segment Needs?

Once you know who the customers are, you need to find out what they want: What are their needs and buying criteria?

What's important to them? Why do they buy? How do they decide?

For example, does one customer segment care a lot about speed of delivery but another cares about order customization? Or does one prefer a premium service while the other prefers better financing terms?

What Is Each Segment's Price Sensitivity?

Next, it's useful to analyze each customer segment's price sensitivity. Not all segments are sensitive to price, so it's useful to know which are—especially in a case where pricing is a key issue.

What Are Each Segment's Distribution Channel Preferences?

A distribution channel, or sales channel, is a company's means of reaching and selling to customers. For example, websites and mail-order catalogs are distribution channels. Selling through a reseller such as Walmart is another, as is having a sales force that visits clients in person.

Different segments of customers prefer to buy through different distribution channels. A client sometimes wants to serve a particular customer segment, but the client's primary distribution channel is one that customers in that segment refuse to use. This conflict needs to be resolved in order for the client to have an effective strategy.

For example, in certain technology markets—such as very expensive software packages—Fortune 500 CIOs prefer to deal with one salesperson per company: one from Sun, one from HP, and one from Apple or IBM. Let's say your client is losing sales because one of its customers is a Fortune 500 company whose CIO wants to deal with one salesperson, but your client is organized into five different divisions, each with its own sales force. So the CIO has to deal with five salespeople and complains, "Not one person from your company knows my entire system. I find that unacceptable, so that's why I'm going with IBM, which has a single person who understands it all."

Sometimes a conflict exists between the channel that the customer would prefer to buy from compared to the channel the company is accustomed to selling through. If such a conflict exists, you want to bring attention to it as a key strategic decision that needs to be resolved. Either the company must change its approach to keep up with evolving customer needs or accept a decline in sales from the customers it's no longer set up to serve.

What Is Each Segment's Customer Concentration?

Customer concentration refers to how many customers exist and how big or small they are. What we're looking for in terms of customer concentration is what I call the *Walmart effect*: It occurs when one big customer (like Walmart) dominates the marketplace and buys products from tens of thousands of manufacturers. (It's very scary when this happens, because that one customer has enormous power over its suppliers.)

In the market you're analyzing, it's useful to know if there are a lot of small customers or only one or two big ones. Even if the total spending is the same, the dynamic can be quite different. Once you know how concentrated the customers are, you want to compare this to the concentration of suppliers (your client's competitors, typically). If an enormous discrepancy in concentration exists between customers and suppliers, then whichever is more concentrated tends to have more power in the industry value chain—the link of relationships between raw-goods provider to manufacturer to retailer to consumer. And quite often the most powerful player in an industry's value chain will benefit economically at the expense of the weakest participants in the value chain.

If customers are more concentrated, then the customers can demand (and get) big price discounts. If suppliers (the client's company and its competitors) are more concentrated, then the vendors in the industry have the power to set high prices, and customers have no choice but to buy at those prices.

By the time I've answered some relevant combination of the five questions I mentioned earlier (as well as any questions inspired by the answers to these questions), I have a good feel for market demand.

Product Analysis

In the product branch of the framework, you look to understand the product at a qualitative level. I use this portion of the framework for market entry or new product introduction cases, in which an understanding of the product itself is critical. If an understanding of the product isn't relevant to the core issue for the client, I skip this section.

Here are the types of questions I consider asking during product analysis:

- What is the nature of the product? (What are its benefits? Why would someone buy it?)

- Is it a commodity good or a unique good? (Could the company increase differentiation?)

- Are there any complementary goods? (Can the company piggyback off growth in complements or near complements?)

- Are there any substitutes? (Is the company vulnerable to indirect competitors, namely substitutes?)

- What is the product's life cycle? (Is it new or almost obsolete?)

- How is it packaged? (This is an optional question. Is anything bundled or included with the product—for example, just a razor versus a razor with replacement blades, or just a product versus a product with a service contract? Would a change in the product's packaging make the product more likely to meet specific consumer segments' needs?)

If you selectively ask questions about these product-related topics, you can uncover insights that will help you refine your hypotheses and ultimately serve your client more effectively.

What Is the Nature of the Product?

I use this type of question to understand the product from a customer's point of view. For example:

- What does the product do?

- Why do people buy it?
- Why is it useful?

Basically, I want to see how the product fits—or doesn't fit—into the customer's world. Is it a nice-to-have product or a must-have?

Ask as many questions as needed until you can clearly visualize how, where, when, and why customers buy and use the product in question.

Is It a Commodity Good or a Unique Good?

The next type of question determines if the product is a commodity product identical across competitors or a unique product. Charging high prices for commodity products while supporting a high profit margin (the percentage of the product's sales price that is profit) is difficult.

The companies that win in commodity markets tend to be large and have incredible operational efficiencies or some type of cost advantage. Walmart is a perfect example of a winner in retail. Company size is a less-relevant factor for unique products as compared to commodity products, so you focus on other factors for unique products to determine which company will win over customers.

Are There Any Complementary Goods?

This type of question helps you determine if other products are (or can be) used in conjunction with the client's product. If your client manufactures peanut butter, you should know that American children often eat jelly on their peanut butter sandwiches. If you sell ketchup, you should know that consumers often dip french fries in ketchup.

Use this type of question to develop strategies for bundling products or partnering with companies in other industries. For example, when I was a child, my mom gave me cheese and crackers as a snack. This involved her cutting up the cheese and putting it in some type of container with some crackers. Someone at a food company noticed children—the customer— eating the company's cheese with crackers. So the company launched an entire line of prepackaged, single-serving snack kits with cheese and crackers in a disposable container. This product has sold well because many moms buy it instead of a big block of cheese, which they have to cut into small pieces.

At the opposite end of the spectrum, for many years General Electric generated more than $20 billion in new revenues by using the same strategy. GE used to be solely a manufacturer of industrial equipment such as jet engines, nuclear power plants, and train locomotives. The company noticed that its customers spent a lot of money to maintain their GE equipment, but because GE didn't offer maintenance services, the customers weren't spending additional money with GE after purchasing the equipment.

To tap into this part of the market, GE began to bundle maintenance contracts, extended warranties, and other repair-type services across all its major product lines. This new offering was wildly successful, bringing in billions of dollars in new revenue, and it all happened because someone at GE was smart enough to figure out what services customers used to complement GE products.

This strategy is especially helpful if the core product is a commodity. If you bundle a commodity product with a unique product, you get a unique bundle that sometimes can be sold for a higher price than the combined price of both products sold independently.

Are There Any Substitutes?

Asking whether there are any substitute products helps you determine what customers are doing if they're not buying your client's product. In this context, *substitute* is another way of saying *indirect competitor*. For example, if the Fortune 500 companies do not buy the latest multimillion-dollar financial analysis software, what do they do instead?

- Do they just use an older system?
- Do they do the computations manually in Excel, even though it takes a lot more time?
- Do they skip the analysis?

Analyzing substitutes for your client's product is useful whenever you encounter a market entry strategy that assumes no competition exists. Having personally entered markets in which there supposedly was no competition, I can tell you that lack of *direct competition* doesn't mean the customer doesn't have *alternatives* to buying your product, which would include the customer just living with his or her problems rather than paying for your product to solve them.

What Is the Product's Life Cycle?

It's useful to evaluate where products—especially technology products—are in their life cycle. If the product is new, can it last in the market for another 20 years? Or is it already in its last year or two of market usefulness?

If you know a product's life cycle, you can time your strategic decisions. A product is at the end of its life cycle when competition is intense, many substitutes exist, and prices have fallen. Rather than invest a lot of money to try to turn around this situation, it might make more sense just to let the product fade away.

Conversely, if the product category is emerging, with decades' more growth ahead of it, making a strategic move within the market rather than exiting the market might be worthwhile—even if competition is intense and substitutes exist. The early years of the smartphone and the tablet computer illustrate this line of thinking perfectly.

How Is It Packaged?

Packaging refers to what products and services are sold together. For example, years ago McDonald's noticed that many customers ordered french fries and a soft drink with their hamburgers, so the restaurant shifted from selling hamburgers to selling "meal deals"—bundles of a hamburger or other sandwich, french fries, and a soft drink. The rest of the fast-food industry shifted dramatically in this direction too because other restaurants discovered that selling meal deals instead of separate items increased sales by 30 percent.

Company Analysis

If your case or hypothesis necessitates a better qualitative understanding of your client's company, you might use the section of the business situation framework on companies. Questions on the following topics can help you identify helpful information about the company that you can then use to refine your hypothesis—and ultimately structure a more customized issue tree:

- Capabilities and expertise
- Distribution channels
- Cost structure (mainly fixed versus variable; is it better to have higher fixed costs with lower variable, which is a barrier to entry, or vice versa?)
- Investment costs (optional: only if the case involves an investment decision)
- Intangibles (e.g., brands, brand loyalty)
- Financial situation
- Organizational structure (optional: if, for example, team organization is in conflict with how customers want to do business, as in the case with the Fortune 500 CIO who wanted to do business with just one person)

Let's review each of these topics in greater depth.

Capabilities and Expertise

You must figure out what the company is good at—its competitive advantages. If I do any company analysis at all, I almost always ask two specific questions related to this topic:

- What does this company do well?
- What does this company do differently than its competitors?

The answers to these two great questions are often very revealing. I love these two questions because you get an awful lot of insightful information from asking *only* two questions—so they're very efficient.

Distribution Channels

You need to know which distribution channels a company uses to sell to its customers. Is it using an e-commerce website or a field sales force? Does it sell through middlemen wholesalers or directly to customers?

Once you understand the company's distribution channel mix (the percentage of sales from each channel), you typically will want to compare it to competitors' distribution channel mixes and customers' distribution channel preferences.

Cost Structure

In the profitability framework, I addressed the importance of understanding a company's ratio of fixed costs to variable costs, especially in comparison to competitors' ratios. I basically extracted the cost portion of the profitability framework and placed it here in the business situation framework. This helps define the strategic options that make sense for the client.

Investment Costs

The case may not involve an investment, but I've added investment costs in this section of the framework as a reminder to consider investment costs when testing the hypothesis. If the primary focus doesn't relate to investment or return on investment, you would typically skip this topic.

Intangibles

You should understand the types of assets the company in the case has to work with. The section of the framework on intangibles reminds you to consider whether intangible assets such as brand names, reputation, and culture are relevant in testing the hypothesis.

For example, if a no-name company and Coca-Cola introduced the exact same beverage, which one would do better in the marketplace? Similarly, much of Apple's fanatical customer following is due to the company's expertise in and reputation for product design.

Financial Situation

No company analysis would be complete without analysis of the company's financial performance. This section of the framework reminds you to analyze both sales and costs— segmented, of course.

Sometimes this analysis isn't relevant—for example, in a new market entry strategy, for which there isn't any historical financial performance to analyze. In such a situation, I skip this analysis, but I always ask myself if financial performance is relevant before I move on.

Organizational Structure

The company's organizational structure can be useful to analyze in cases that involve an execution aspect. Most cases deal with a big strategic decision—not the execution of a previously made decision—so you likely won't need to consider this topic during the case interview.

As a working consultant, however, you would be wise to analyze the company's organizational structure to identify any conflicts between the structure and the strategy. We can refer again to the Fortune 500 CIO for this topic: If the CIO will deal with only one point of contact, he will not want to work with a company organized into five divisions, each with its own sales force.

Competition Analysis

An analysis of the competition involves looking at the following:

- Competitor concentration and structure (monopoly, oligopoly, competitive, market share concentration)
- Competitor behaviors (customer segments, products, pricing strategy, distribution strategy, brand loyalty)
- Best practices (whether they're doing things the client is not)
- Barriers to entry (whether the client should be concerned about new entrants to market)

- Supplier concentration (optional: e.g., Microsoft or Intel in the PC market)
- Regulatory environment

Competitor Concentration and Structure

Knowing how many competitors a company has and how big they are is extremely useful. Let's say that all a company's competitors combined have $1 billion in annual sales. Does the competition consist of one company that generated $1 billion in sales, or does it consist of 100,000 competitors that each generated $10,000 in sales? The former indicates that the competition is a monopoly with high concentration, and the latter means the competition is highly fragmented.

If you understand the revenue concentration in a few key competitors (or the lack thereof), you get a sense of how much power these competitors possess. Power typically comes from two places: (1) a dramatically lower cost structure that can support lowering prices while maintaining profitability, and (2) a concentration so high that customers have no alternatives (competitor can raise prices and "force" customers to buy because they have few or no other choices).

The more concentrated the competition, the more you have to worry about it. If you don't realize when a case involves high competitor concentration, you could easily make a strategic recommendation that's flat-out wrong. The easiest way to assess competitor concentration is to ask the following questions:

- How many competitors are there?
- How big are they (in terms of sales or market share)?

Competitor Behaviors

Answer these questions:

- What strategic choices do key competitors make?
- Who are their customers?
- What products do they offer?
- What distribution channels do they use?

If you forget what questions to ask, use the question list from the business situation framework's company and product sections—but instead of applying it to your client, apply it to the competitor. (Note how I reuse a single framework in many different ways, which means there's less for me to memorize.)

You need to identify competitors' strategic choices so you can compare them to your client's strategic choices and to how the customer segments have evolved over time.

As I've mentioned, a single piece of information isn't often very useful by itself—comparing it to something else increases its utility. Once you know what top competitors are doing, you can compare that information to your findings from both your customer and company analyses.

Best Practices

If your client isn't winning in the marketplace, ask, "What is the competitor doing that we aren't?" Once you learn the answer, you don't necessarily have your client copy that behavior. Sometimes the competitor exploits some inherent competitive advantage in order to engage in a particular best practice. Instead, decide whether your client can compete.

If your client can't beat the competitor in its area of strength, one strategic option is to refocus your client's business on a competitor's weakness. If the competitor sells at the lowest prices, has the lowest cost structure, and is realistically unbeatable at the low-price game, you could position your client as the high-priced, highest-quality provider instead.

Sometimes clients can pull away from competitors by doing the opposite of what those competitors do. This isn't always a good idea, but it makes sense at least to *know* what competitors are doing well so you can *consider* doing the same or the polar opposite.

Barriers to Entry

If a competitor has created something difficult or expensive to copy, it tends to erect barriers to entry and thus discourage competition. For example, the enormous pharmaceutical companies have many barriers to entry, including huge research and development budgets to fund two decades' worth of research to bring a single drug to market, and a global sales force that sells new drugs.

For a new company to compete with established players, it has to either beat these companies in research and development or in sales, or find an entirely different way to compete. If you know what barriers to entry competitors possess, you can determine another entry plan that makes more sense.

Supplier Concentration

Sometimes understanding how much power an industry's suppliers have provides a context for interpreting competitors' behavior. The key here is to determine how concentrated or fragmented the suppliers are. If many suppliers all do a pretty good job, that means it's a competitive market that you don't have to worry too much about. But if the suppliers are highly concentrated or if one supplier has a monopoly, take heed.

If your client's supplier is Microsoft, for example, you'll need to examine the relationship carefully, because in many markets Microsoft has a monopoly and wields enormous power.

Sometimes competitors do things to serve customers better, and other times they do things in reaction to what competitors do. But there's another scenario that sometimes catches people off guard: Sometimes a competitor will act in response to the dictates of a handful of powerful suppliers.

Regulatory Environment

Some heavily regulated industries are prohibited from engaging in certain activities that might otherwise make sense for a company. You need to be aware of these existing restrictions and to pay particularly close attention to recent changes in the regulatory environment.

It's quite common for such changes to restrict certain, and in some cases commonplace, activities, thereby forcing every company in the industry to adapt. In other cases, a more restrictive regulatory change might shift the attractiveness of whatever activities are still permitted, turning what used to be a borderline-attractive opportunity into a more attractive one for the sole reason that there's no other choice. Changes in the regulatory environment also create opportunities—opening the door for companies to engage in new activities that weren't previously permissible. In these instances, existing companies accustomed to the status quo are often slow to realize the possibilities.

Practical Tips for Using the Business Situation Framework

About 50 percent of the time, I don't finish the entire business situation framework. By the time I've worked through part of the framework, I usually discover some key insight that gives me a feel for what's really going on in a case. Once this happens, no matter where I am in the framework, I immediately synthesize, revise my hypothesis, and determine what is the *least* amount of information I need to test my revised hypothesis.

Sometimes all I need is an abbreviated version of the rest of the business situation framework. Other times I pluck out just one of the four major branches: customer, product, company, or competitor. And even within one of the major branches, I might skip more than half the questions.

I've listed the questions above for each branch of the business situation in order of how often I use them. If I plan to analyze a branch, I almost always ask the first one or two questions in each of the four major categories, and I rarely ask the last question in each category. You're not supposed to—nor do you have the time to—ask every question in every area.

Opening the case with these standard questions will feel mechanical, but it's because of these questions that the interviewer will share useful information with you, so be sure to listen carefully.

If you go through the framework so mechanically that the only thing you're doing is trying to remember the next question, you'll likely miss any insightful information the interviewer might mention, or more realistically, you'll hear what the interviewer says but be too preoccupied to notice a statement's significance.

I'll close this chapter by reiterating a key theme: The purpose of a framework is *not* to complete the framework by the end of the interview. The purpose is to test a hypothesis. The business situation framework will give you a better qualitative understanding of the situation, help you refine your hypothesis, and help you find increasingly efficient ways to test it.

Chapter 15

MERGERS AND ACQUISITIONS FRAMEWORK

THE MERGERS AND acquisitions (M&A) framework is quite straightforward, and you'll use it when Company A is deciding if Company B is the right one to acquire or merge with.

This framework helps determine the *conceptual reasons* for acquiring another company. It doesn't calculate financial return-on-investment figures or mathematically calculate changes in industry production capacity (sometimes it makes sense to buy a competitor in order to shut it down) as a way to boost industry prices. If you get a case involving financial return on investment, use a custom issue tree.

The M&A framework is simply a variation of the business situation framework and thus addresses the same four key components that we need to understand about a business: customers, products, company, and competition. The M&A framework, however, analyzes each of these areas twice — once for each company in the potential M&A transaction.

After you analyze each company independently, you'll run a third analysis of the two companies combined, which will provide you with qualitative insights about the benefits of such a transaction. Once you run all the analyses, you would use the qualitative data to refine your hypothesis and then analyze the potential benefits quantitatively (e.g., estimate the magnitude of financial benefit).

The most common M&A cases center on either strategic value or cost savings. The premise of a strategic value deal is that the combination of the two companies creates something more than either company could achieve on its own. A classic example of such a transaction is when Company A, a huge company with the biggest sales force on Earth, wants to acquire Company B, a small company that has a hot, brand-new product but very limited sales distribution. The rationale is that you move the product from Company B to Company A, let the large sales force work its magic, and boom! The new company has the hottest product on the market and the best distribution.

In the cost savings deal, the new company combines the two companies in order to "eliminate" a negative (in this case, costs).

The primary difference between these two types of deals is the duration of the benefits. Strategic value deals tend to extend benefits over the long term, and cost savings deals realize benefits immediately and just once. After the savings are realized, the ongoing value of the deal is less (typically the cost savings will persist, though rarely grow, over time).

Chapter 16

FRAMEWORKS IN ACTION

I'VE SAID IT before, and I'll say it again: Use frameworks and issue trees flexibly. For example, use one framework to discover as much as possible and then switch to another framework to conduct more analysis or test your hypothesis. The following scenario illustrates how to flexibly apply the frameworks discussed in previous chapters in the context of a candidate-led case—a case format I'll elaborate on in Part Five.

Omega & Omega is a billion-dollar advertising agency that serves only Fortune 500 accounts. Its sales have remained unchanged over the past three years. The company has asked for your advice on *how to grow its profits* and *sales.*

Candidate: Our client Omega & Omega appears to be a billion-dollar agency with flat sales and profits. The client is looking for us to help grow sales and profits. Is that right?

(In the opening of a case, write down and confirm the client's specific goal. Candidates commonly and mistakenly interchange sales with profits. A company that wants to grow profits wants something completely different than does one that cares only about growing sales. Many candidates hear the word grow *and automatically assume the client wants to grow only sales or only profits. Never assume. Always listen* carefully and always *double-check that you heard correctly.)*

Candidate: This is a pretty broad problem, so I'd like to start with an arbitrary hypothesis. Because the client wants both sales and profits to increase, let's hypothesize that the client has a sales growth problem. To test that hypothesis, I'd like to break down the client's profits into its component parts: sales and costs. Specifically, I'd like to understand how each has changed in the past three years, because we know that's the duration in which sales and profits have remained flat.

(I opted to start with the profitability framework to better isolate whether the problem is due to cost or revenue. My hope is that this initial analysis will help me figure out what problem the client needs us to solve. Although I started this case with the profitability framework, I may not end the case with it.)

Interviewer: The business has been profitable during the past three years. Revenues and costs have remained unchanged during this time.

Candidate: OK, things have remained flat during this time. I wonder if this is an industry-wide problem or a company-specific problem. Is comparable data for the rest of the industry available?

(You want to do two things when you analyze most company performance metrics: Compare a metric (1) across different historical time periods, and (2) with the rest of the industry. The first comparison will help you discover any triggering event that may have caused the client's headache, and the second comparison will help you determine whether the key issue is industry-wide or company-specific. You can efficiently narrow the problem by making these comparisons.)

Interviewer: The rest of the industry has seen both sales and profits grow by 10 percent during this time.

Candidate: The rest of the industry appears to have grown sales by 10 percent, with profits growing proportionally. This indicates that the industry-wide profit margin percentages have remained unchanged and that the primary driver of increased profits is sales growth. It also suggests the rest of the industry has not undertaken any major cost-reduction initiatives. If we solve the sales problem for the client, the data suggests that the profit problem will solve itself.

In addition, because cutting costs will not automatically boost sales, growing sales — with all other variables unchanged — will automatically boost profits, so it makes sense to focus on growing sales and circle back to cutting costs, if necessary, to achieve the client's objective.

Our goal now is to figure out what the rest of the industry is doing that our client isn't to grow sales.

(Notice how much clearer the problem is now than it was at the opening of the case. The opening dealt with how to grow sales and profits, and now I've narrowed the focus to figuring out what the rest of the industry is doing that the client isn't to grow. I was able to get to this much more specific point in a minute or two just by asking some of the right questions. Also, notice that I asked each question for a specific reason. Some candidates, unfortunately, ask dozens of questions without a concrete objective in mind.)

Interviewer: OK, sounds like a plan. How would you like to proceed?

Candidate: Well, I'd like to know the components of revenue. For example, do we know if there's a change in revenue per account or in the number of accounts?

Interviewer: The number of accounts has remained constant, and the average billings per account has remained unchanged.

Candidate: That's interesting. No real change, huh? Our client seems to be maintaining the status quo. Meanwhile, the rest of the industry is experiencing some kind of growth—either more accounts or more billings per account. Is comparable data for the rest of the industry available?

Interviewer: Yes, it is. The number of large advertisers has not changed for the rest of the industry. The aggregate spending of each advertiser across all agencies has increased.

Candidate: OK, so clearly customer demand is up. Other competitors are stepping in to fill that demand, but our client is not.

(At this point, I'm thinking, "What the hell is going on here? Something's weird.")

Candidate: I sense we're just missing something critical. *Something* is causing this to happen. Either customers have changed in a way that has benefited our competitors but not our client, or competitors have changed in a way that attracts new business but we haven't.

(Note how I framed the issue in concrete terms: Either competitors or customers have changed. Laying out an issue in this structured way makes it easier for the interviewer to follow your logic. I could just as easily have said, "I think we need to look into the customers themselves," or I could have started asking questions about customers. The problem with diving in this way is that it doesn't give the interviewer any insight into the organization of your thought process. Are you asking questions like a reporter would, or are you asking questions for a specific purpose?

By framing the issue to determine whether customers or competitors have changed, you make it clear that to solve this mystery, you need to understand both of these areas — and remember to state why that understanding is critical. If you fail to mention why, you'll lose points in the case interview for failing to communicate the logical rationale behind your approach.

One of these two things, or perhaps both, is happening, and in order to make a recommendation to the client, I need to understand these two areas better. Because the profitability framework won't give me the additional information I need about customers and competitors, I've officially exhausted its usefulness. My working hypothesis has evolved and the current framework doesn't cover the data needed to test that hypothesis, so it's time to switch frameworks. I could stick with the profitability framework and force in questions about customers and competitors, but I'd get disorganized quickly.)

Candidate: To better understand what's going on for Omega & Omega and its industry, we need to look at four key areas: the customers, the products, the company itself, and the competitors.

(In this particular situation, it would be reasonable to do a custom issue tree for customers, the company, and competitors. If I were to take this approach, I would drill down into competitors first and then customers, because I already know a bit about the company. What I don't know is whether the competitors are doing something the client isn't.

So why not start with customers, which I usually suggest? When any other information is missing, I start with customers, but in this case, I know that competitors are doing something the client isn't. For the sake of time, it's important to figure out as soon as possible what that something *is. Realistically, I won't know why the competitor made certain changes unless I understand the customers. With limited time, I find it slightly more useful to know what the competitor is doing differently instead of* why.

Whether you start with customers or competitors, be sure to justify why you chose one over the other. You want to demonstrate that you considered the decision carefully, not just flipped a coin.

Also keep in mind that certain decisions just don't make sense and are therefore "wrong." For example, in this case, it doesn't make sense to start with the product, because this is primarily a "what is my competitor doing that I'm not doing?" case. Understanding the details of what the product is and how it works isn't the next most important issue, but that doesn't mean those details might not be important or that the relative importance of products might not change with new information. Even if you learn about the industry's products, you still don't know what competitors have done. Plus, analyzing the product doesn't tell you what the client should do.

Do consultants really think about all this in the middle of a conversation or interview? Yes. Do you need to master this way of thinking right away? No. Should you work on being more thoughtful in your decisions during a case interview? Absolutely.

My main point here is that you need to rationalize and argue for why you want to start the case in one place instead of another. No matter where you start, you must show you've considered your choice carefully.)

Candidate: My hypothesis is that some segment of the industry is growing and our competitors are participating in that segment, but for some reason we are not. The data indicates that competitors are doing something differently than our client, so I'd like to start there. Then I'll analyze the customers so that we can better understand the underlying trends our competitors might be responding to. Next, I'll uncover key differences and opportunities by comparing all that to the client's operations. I'll save the product for last, just in case we discover any new product innovation that might be relevant.

To test the hypothesis that the competitors are targeting some segment of the market that our client is not, we need to answer some questions: Who are the competitors? What are the major categories of competitors? How much market share does each type of competitor category have of the total market?

Interviewer: Well, there are four types of advertising agencies: global ad agencies, direct response agencies, digital advertising agencies, and media-buying agencies.

Candidate: What is a direct response agency?

Interviewer: It does direct mail.

Candidate: Oh, OK, got it. Digital advertising agencies— they sort of do online advertising, is that right?

Interviewer: Yes, that's right.

Candidate: What's this media-buying thing?

Interviewer: Well, the ad business tends to split into two groups: people who create ads and people who buy ad space. Each of the groups has its own specialists.

Candidate: Got it. What percentage of the total market does each category of competitor represent?

Interviewer: Let's say global advertising represents 50 percent, direct response 20 percent, online 10 percent, and media buying 20 percent.

Candidate: How many agencies are in the biggest segment, global advertising?

Interviewer: Four or five.

Candidate: OK, so it's a very concentrated industry among the global agencies. How concentrated are the other segments of competitors?

Interviewer: The other segments have dozens, and in some cases hundreds, of competitors.

Candidate: Compared to the global ad segment, how big are the competitors in the direct response, media-buying, and online segments?

Interviewer: They are significantly smaller.

Candidate: OK, so a few big players control half the market, and a bunch of smaller players participate in the other half of the market. Next, given my hypothesis that our client is missing out on some segment of the market, I'd like to better understand which types of competitors are growing—the global ad agencies, media-buying agencies, direct response agencies, or digital agencies.

Interviewer: Over the past three years, the global ad agencies as a group have experienced a slight decline in sales and profits, the direct response and media-buying agencies have experienced flat sales and profits, and the sales and profits of the digital advertising agencies have grown 60 percent per year.

Candidate: Aha! Interesting. So industry growth is really being driven by a single segment that is offsetting flat and declining sales in other segments.

(Note the effective use of a mini-synthesis.)

Candidate: Given this circumstance, my revised hypothesis is that to jump-start growth, Omega & Omega has to find some way to participate in the only market segment that's growing: digital advertising. To test this hypothesis, we have to figure out what's driving growth for digital agencies and determine if it's a long-term trend or just a temporary one. And we need to figure out if the client can find a way to benefit from this trend.

(Thanks to this "aha" discovery, I now understand what's going on with the competitors. Now I need to know why digital advertising is growing so fast, which is the key to testing my hypothesis. Because of this, the unanswered questions from the competitors section of the business situation framework—such as questions on best practices, barriers to entry, and supplier concentration—aren't as critical as figuring out why digital advertising is growing. To understand this, we need to understand the cause of growth: customers.)

Candidate: Because digital advertising is the only segment that's growing, we need to understand more about what's going on with customers, so I'm going to switch gears and analyze customers next.

Interviewer: That sounds like a reasonable plan. Why don't you go ahead and do that.

Candidate: I'd like to know who these customers are. What are the key customer segments? What's the growth rate of each segment?

Interviewer: Well, the customers are Fortune 500 brand managers such as Procter & Gamble, midmarket-size clients, and small-business clients.

Candidate: OK, that's interesting. And what percentage of total industry ad dollars does each segment represent?

Interviewer: The big P&G kind of companies are spending 70 percent of all advertising dollars, midmarket companies 20 percent, and small businesses 10 percent.

Candidate: Well, this is really interesting. So far we've established that digital advertising is the spending category that's growing, and the most recent information shows us that the big companies spend the most on advertising. My hypothesis is that the big companies are the ones shifting toward digital advertising in their marketing plans. To test this, I need to see a breakdown of advertising spending for the big companies over the past three years. Are the big companies the ones driving spending in digital advertising?

Interviewer: Let's say the total ad spend by big companies is $4 billion out of a total of $5.7 billion across all advertisers annually. Of that $4 billion, big companies spent $3.4 billion on a combination of global brand advertising, media buying, and direct response, with the remaining $600 million going toward digital advertising. Three years ago, big companies spent $3.4 billion on a combination of brand advertising, media buying, and direct response, and $150 million on digital advertising.

Candidate: So Fortune 500 companies' increased investment in digital advertising over the past three years seems to have driven the bulk of the industry's growth. This trend has contributed approximately $450 million in growth over the last three years. We know that this $5.7 billion industry has grown by roughly 10 percent, or $570 million, over the past three years. So the increase in digital advertising appears to represent approximately 80 percent of industry-wide growth.

At this point, I think we have a pretty clear idea what's happening among the competitors, and we have some initial insights into customers as well. We know that the bulk of the industry's growth comes from the digital advertising segment, whose core customer is the large company. Based on this, my working hypothesis is that Omega & Omega must participate more effectively in this market segment if it wants to grow.

In addition, because the digital advertisers are the same advertisers that represent Omega & Omega's core client base, Omega & Omega's failure to establish a stronger presence in this segment poses a long-term risk that the company's relationship with its core clients will become vulnerable to agencies with stronger digital capabilities. To test this hypothesis further, I want to analyze customers in more detail.

Interviewer: OK, how would you like to proceed?

Candidate: I'd like to start by learning more about what each customer segment is looking for in an agency. Then I want to see if Omega & Omega has been able to give these types of clients what they're looking for.

Interviewer: Well, the Fortune 500 companies historically have focused on traditional media such as print, television, and radio. In traditional media, the advertiser is looking to build brand awareness, up the creativity factor, and establish an emotional connection with the consumer. Traditional media accounts for roughly 85 percent of a Fortune 500 company's advertising budget.

A newer area for these advertisers is digital advertising. In this area, the objectives seem to differ. Because the medium is so data-rich, the advertisers are looking for a concrete return on investment that they can measure in quantitative terms rather than intuitive ones. Digital advertising currently represents 15 percent of the Fortune 500 companies' overall marketing budget.

Candidate: May I interrupt? You've indicated an interesting trend whereby large advertisers split their spending between traditional advertising and digital advertising. Before we go further into customer analysis, I'd like to compare this information we've just discovered about large advertisers to our client's mix of business. What percentage of Omega & Omega's business is traditional advertising versus digital advertising?

Interviewer: Omega & Omega derives 98 percent of its revenues from traditional advertising and only 2 percent from digital advertising.

Candidate: Interesting. Well, the problem appears to be that Omega & Omega is really strong in the area that customers care less and less about. Traditional advertising is a big segment today, but growth is clearly shifting toward digital advertising, further supporting the hypothesis that Omega & Omega's presence in the digital advertising market lags behind customers' spending habits in that market.

I'd like to learn more about each customer segment's sensitivity to pricing. How does the pricing work, and who's willing to pay what?

Interviewer: In traditional brand advertising, ad agencies charge a fee that's a percentage of the overall media budget, typically 15 percent of the total media spend. In digital advertising, ad agencies charge 20 percent of total media spend as their fee.

Candidate: Ah, interesting. This suggests that digital advertising might be more profitable. Is any cost data on that available?

Interviewer: We don't have precise data on that, but our understanding is that labor costs are 15 percent higher on the digital side per $1 million in campaign spending.

Candidate: Do the decision makers at Omega & Omega's clients also decide on spending for digital advertising?

Interviewer: Yes.

Candidate: Given that pricing is 33 percent higher for digital advertising (20 percent commissions for digital ads versus 15 percent commissions for traditional ads), it more than offsets the 15 percent higher labor costs, suggesting that profit margins in digital advertising might be higher than they are in traditional advertising. This further supports the hypothesis that digital advertising is an attractive market segment for Omega & Omega.

(By now I'm thinking that perhaps consumers shifting toward Internet media are driving this spending trend. Given this intuitive opinion derived from personal experience, it would be appropriate to state this as a hypothesis and attempt to validate it with data. It would not be appropriate to assume automatically and without confirming with facts that this is true.)

Candidate: Advertisers are shifting their budgets aggressively into digital advertising. Does any information explain why the advertisers are doing this?

Interviewer: Advertisers have noticed consumers shifting their media consumption away from TV, print, and radio and toward Internet media. TV, print, and radio consumption is on a slight decline, and consumer Internet media usage has grown extremely aggressively.

Candidate: It sounds like we're seeing a structural shift in media consumption patterns among consumers. In response, advertisers are shifting their advertising dollars toward online media. This, in turn, has caused the advertising agency's digital advertising service providers to grow at the expense of the rest of the industry—including Omega & Omega.

So now we have to answer a few questions: What do we do about it? What do we have to work with? What assets do we have? Once we answer these questions, we can determine how Omega & Omega could participate in this market more effectively. To do this, I'd like to understand Omega & Omega's operations better.

(I am now shifting to the company branch of the business situation framework. I've uncovered data to establish the working hypothesis that

digital advertising is attractive and growing, but I haven't determined what Omega & Omega should do about it, so I need to discover more data about the company in order to develop a more specific recommendation.)

Candidate: I'd like to know more about the company's capabilities and expertise. In other words, what is the company good at?

Interviewer: Omega & Omega is quite good at creating blockbuster television ads. The company is strong on creative, branding, slogans, and jingles.

Candidate: How does Omega & Omega access its customers? What kind of distribution channel does it use?

Interviewer: In terms of distribution, Omega & Omega has a direct sales force that's constantly contacting the Fortune 500 accounts.

Candidate: Do Fortune 500 buyers prefer to buy via an in-person sales force?

Interviewer: Yes.

Candidate: This is interesting. It seems the sales force at Omega & Omega is already in contact with the Fortune 500 decision makers who authorize investments in digital advertising. Despite this access, the customer still chooses to buy from another agency instead. Do the customers indicate why they prefer to buy elsewhere?

Interviewer: Yes, they say that when they want to make a big brand introduction or reposition a brand, they call creativity-driven companies such as Omega & Omega. But when it comes to digital advertising, they need an advertising agency to deliver quantifiable results—increased number of orders, increased number of visits to the store, etc. They feel that Omega & Omega lacks skills and a track record in this area.

Candidate: Let me take a shot at recapping where we are. A mismatch exists between Omega & Omega's abilities and what customers want in return for money spent in the fastest-growing segment of the market: digital advertising. In this area, advertisers want online ads with really good metrics — basically, statistics-driven marketing. Unfortunately, Omega & Omega is good at creativity-driven marketing only.

Interviewer: So what do you tell Omega & Omega to do?

Candidate: Well, that's a big challenge. Omega & Omega is facing a structural shift in market demand: The segments in which Omega & Omega excels are shrinking, and the segments in which it lacks skill and experience are growing incredibly fast. So Omega & Omega isn't positioned properly in the marketplace relative to new market demand. In terms of recommendations, Omega & Omega needs to be where the demand is if it wants to grow. The company has two options: Build that capability internally or buy it externally. Omega & Omega has tried the former, so I think it should seriously consider an acquisition.

Interviewer: Interesting insight. Given this skills mismatch, how should Omega & Omega go about evaluating acquisition candidates?

(For demonstration purposes, I've deliberately created this case to lead into an M&A case. Notice that something as simple as an interviewer asking an off-the-cuff question can send a case in a new direction, necessitating new frameworks or issue trees. This happens fairly often, so you might as well get used to the idea and be flexible.

Before I evaluate various acquisition candidates, I need to identify my decision-making criteria. Based on my analysis, Omega & Omega should focus on acquisition targets that:

- *Provide Omega & Omega with capabilities, capacity, and credibility in digital advertising.*
- *Have a sales force with the reach, skills, and track record to sell effectively to Omega & Omega's Fortune 500 client contacts.*
- *Can immediately increase Omega & Omega's U.S. sales and profit, preferably without cannibalizing existing sales.*

My first steps would be to identify a short list of candidates, analyze each target, and ultimately narrow the list to a few candidates worth considering. I would want to get a market share breakdown of all the companies in the digital advertising segment. I would focus first on the companies with at least $1 billion in sales, because that amount would add meaningful revenue growth to Omega & Omega.

Let's jump back into the case interview.)

Candidate: Do we have a market share breakdown of the digital advertising segment?

Interviewer: This segment has three dominant competitors: eCool Advertising, Super Click, and MathAds. Together, they generate around $400 million in revenue, or roughly 66 percent of the market. The remaining 34 percent of the market is highly fragmented, with market share split across 100 much smaller firms.

Candidate: What does the market share structure look like?

Interviewer: eCool generates $200 million a year in sales, Super Click $100 million, MathAds $100 million, and everybody else combined $200 million. eCool is the most dominant player of the top three. Super Click and MathAds are basically midlevel players. The group of smaller firms picks up all the pieces the other three don't get.

Candidate: Well, among the potential targets, the three market share leaders make the most sense to consider first. If the top three targets weren't promising, then it would make sense to circle back to consider whether any of the much smaller firms might be a good fit.

Interviewer: Great, that sounds pretty reasonable to me. How would you go about evaluating each of the three companies?

(This is where I would transition to the M&A framework. To do this, I would use the business situation framework for each target company on its own and then mentally combine each target company's assets, both financial and nonfinancial, with Omega & Omega's to see how the combined entity would stack up across customers, competitors,

company, and product. To facilitate this comparison, I'd make a table in my notes that lists Customers, Competitors, Company, and Product as the column headings, with each target company's name occupying its own row in the leftmost column. Once I've assembled all this information, I can use the table to compare the target companies and determine whether they'd be a good fit with Omega & Omega.)

Candidate: So let's start with customer analysis for all the potential targets and for Omega & Omega. Who are the customers of each potential target? What do these customers want?

Interviewer: As stated previously, Omega & Omega serves Fortune 500 accounts, typically at the level of chief marketing officer. eCool serves the same types of accounts almost exclusively, but it emphasizes digital advertising instead of traditional advertising. Super Click's and MathAds' accounts comprise 60 percent Fortune 500 and 40 percent midmarket. In addition, 50 percent of Super Click's sales come from Europe.

Candidate: Among the Fortune 500 accounts that each company serves, do they serve different industry segments or types of accounts? Or is their mix of Fortune 500 accounts fairly similar?

Interviewer: Let's assume that within the Fortune 500 accounts, the client mix is similar in terms of industry, size of company, and geography within the United States.

Candidate: So from a customer focus standpoint, eCool seems to be the leading candidate so far. My initial hypothesis is that eCool is the most attractive target and its revenues are greatest overall. Considering only the U.S. market, eCool is twice as large as MathAds and four times larger than Super Click. eCool also leads in the number of Fortune 500 accounts, with roughly three times as many as both Super Click and MathAds in this customer segment.

To test this hypothesis further, I'd like to learn more about how the firms' products and services differ. What does each company sell? Do they all provide something similar, or do some of the companies offer something different? Does one company focus on a specialized type of work, whereas others are more general? Does one offer low-end products and services and the others high-end products and services? Do we know of any major distinctions across the three companies?

Interviewer: We can assume that the products and services each of these companies sells are comparable to the other companies'. All the companies provide advertising consultation services, creative development, and campaign execution services, and all are well-respected.

Candidate: This further reinforces the hypothesis that eCool is the strongest potential target. To continue to test this hypothesis, I'd like to compare the three companies in terms of their internal operations. In terms of their financial performance, does any one firm outperform the others once you adjust for size? For example, do their profit margin percentages vary by much?

Interviewer: eCool's financial performance in dollars is roughly double that of Super Click and MathAds. In terms of financial ratios, all the firms perform at similar levels.

Candidate: I see. Do the companies have the same capabilities or distribution channels?

Interviewer: All three companies share similar capabilities and go-to-market approaches.

Candidate: I see. This suggests that, revenue size aside, the firms do not differ materially in terms of financial performance, capabilities, and go-to-market approach.

Interviewer: Given the information available to you, what recommendation would you make to the client, and why?

Candidate: Omega & Omega should focus its expansion efforts in digital advertising via acquisition, with eCool as the leading candidate. I base this conclusion on these three reasons:

- Digital advertising is growing 60 percent per year in an otherwise stagnant industry.

- Omega & Omega lags significantly in the digital advertising segment and lacks the internal skills to grow in this segment.

- eCool is the largest digital advertising player, with a size advantage over the other two target companies that is two to four times greater in the U.S.-based Fortune 500 account segment, which Omega & Omega highly values.

For these reasons, Omega & Omega should expand into the fast-growing digital advertising segment by acquiring a company such as eCool.

* * *

Throughout this case interview example, the candidate's hypothesis—or hunch—drives the direction of the case. The candidate uses different frameworks as appropriate to test the prevailing hypothesis—not the other way around—which is exactly what you should do in your own case interviews.

The next several chapters cover how to apply these foundational case interviewing skills to a variety of case interview formats. Each case format requires identical fundamental skills, but how you apply these skills varies a little depending on the format.

* * *

For additional sample cases, you may want to reference my Look Over My Shoulder program. It's a program that contains audio recordings of case interviews with 20+ candidates of varying skill levels. It also includes commentary on what distinguishes poor, good, and exceptional responses to case questions. For more information, visit www.caseinterview.com/jump/loms.

PART FIVE

The Candidate-Led Case

Chapter 17

HOW TO OPEN A CANDIDATE-LED CASE

THIS SECTION COVERS the classic candidate-led case interview format—a format used by the consulting industry for decades. By mastering the fundamentals of this case format, you'll do well with any other format too. Subsequent chapters cover the other case formats, using the candidate-led format as a reference point

Overview

In a candidate-led case, the candidate drives the case process. You're in charge, so you decide in which direction you want to go. To candidates, this format is the most unstructured and ambiguous. For example, let's say an interviewer asks you, "Should Airline X close down service in ten of its markets?" After that, he'll literally shut his mouth for the next 35 minutes unless you ask him a question or request some data.

In high school, I always found multiple-choice questions, which have a fixed number of possible answers to choose from, easy for two reasons: First, the number of possible answers was finite. Second, the answer was already printed right on the test page (though I still had to recognize it). This type of question is a closed question—it has a simple A, B, C, or D answer.

I never enjoyed taking tests, but I certainly preferred the multiple-choice format to the dreaded essay question: "Compare and contrast this literary work to that literary work. Limit: Five pages." I found that type of open-ended question much more difficult to answer because you actually had to know what you were talking about.

As it turns out, the candidate-led case interview process is an incredibly open-ended one, which is why many consulting firms use it. It mirrors (perfectly, I might add) how clients present questions to consulting firms. Firms that want consultants who can structure the highly ambiguous find this format useful in evaluating this specific skill area.

I think many firms have stopped relying on this format exclusively because, although it tests a candidate's problem-structuring skills extremely well, it doesn't necessarily test skills in collaboration, presentation, or math. Most firms use this classic case format in addition to other formats in order to evaluate a candidate's abilities more comprehensively.

How to Start?

At the beginning of a case, you're given very little information—perhaps a sentence or two. You know the client's in trouble, but what do you do? You have no data.

Part of the initial challenge is to request the right data, in the right order, from the interviewer. The order in which you ask for data should be based on logic, not on a scattershot approach in which you ask for all kinds of data without a coherent, rational motivation for your requests.

Why is a logical order important to interviewers? Because it's important to consultants every day. Clients tell consultants, "I'm in trouble. I need help with X. What do I do? I have 45,000 employees, and you can interview any of them. Who do you want to interview? I have billions of records of information in my database, and you can look at anything you want. Oh yeah, by the way, I can afford to pay your team for only four weeks. So where do you want to start?" As a working consultant, you're *always* under time and resource constraints. A deliberate, logical approach is essential to surviving as a consultant. As a result, consulting firms look for this ability in their candidates.

Below are five practical steps to open a case:

Step #1: Stall!

The first thing I do when opening a case is *stall*. I'm serious about this. Let's say the client (think of the interviewer as your client) asks, "Should I acquire my biggest competitor?" I always say, "Hmmm, that's an interesting question," pause silently for about five seconds, and repeat the question s-l-o-w-l-y. "So, you want to know if you should acquire your biggest competitor?" The interviewer says yes, of course. After you've paused, repeated the question, heard the interviewer's response, and paused again, you've gained an extra 20 to 30 seconds to think.

Why is this important? Because despite the facts that I've been the candidate in more than 60 case interviews and my clients have asked me hundreds of case-like questions over the years, about 50 percent of the time my instinctive initial reaction to such serious questions still is to say, "I have no freaking idea!"

Stalling allows that brief moment of panic to subside so I can consider whether a case sounds similar to any other case I've encountered. If I've worked through a similar case, how did I structure it? Which parts of the current case seem different? Can I use a standard framework or do I need a custom issue tree? Which would be a better fit? If a standard framework is the better fit, is there anything unusual about this case that would prompt me to consider modifying that framework (e.g., using only half the framework because the other half isn't relevant)?

It's impossible to answer all these questions in only one second, but you can answer a good number of them by stalling for 20 to 30 seconds and following the rest of the steps below.

Step #2: Clarify Your Understanding

Next, you need to verify your understanding of facts and terminology, because the same word can mean something different from industry to industry. For example:

Interviewer: The CEO of a reinsurance company is concerned because premiums are down 15 percent. What do you tell the client to do?

(*I'm really thinking to myself,* Hmmm, that's an interesting question, but what the hell is reinsurance?)

Candidate: Can I ask some background questions before I get started?

Interviewer: Sure.

Candidate: What's reinsurance?

Interviewer: It's insurance for insurance companies.

Candidate: Oh, OK.

Interviewer: For example, insurance companies have insurance policies on their homeowners' policies. So if the insurance companies lose a combined $2 billion in claims from, say, a single natural disaster in Florida, the reinsurance company pays the portion of the loss that exceeds $2 billion.

Candidate: Ah, OK. So it's insurance for insurance companies, I get that. Next question: What's a premium? Is that like profits?

Interviewer: No, it's like revenues. A premium is what people pay every month to get insurance. A company's premiums are the aggregate of all the clients' individual premiums.

Candidate: So basically you're saying the client is asking me what to do because revenues are down 15 percent. Is that right?

Interviewer: Yes.

Asking just a few clarifying questions ensures that I understand the client's situation and the *specific question* I need to answer. Quite a few candidates don't pass a case interview because they misunderstand the client's situation or objective. *Don't make that mistake!*

Step #3: Stall Again!

Once you're sure you understand the client's situation and objective, ask, "Is it OK if I take a minute to organize my thoughts?" Take the next 30 to 60 seconds to do steps 4 and 5: State your hypothesis and structure your case.

Under the stress of an interview, most people have difficulty estimating how much time has passed. To a slightly stressed-out candidate, 10 seconds of silence can easily feel like 30 seconds, and 60 seconds of someone staring at you in silence while you're writing notes can feel like 10 minutes.

So how can you gauge how much time has really passed? I recommend practicing. Have a friend stare at you like an interviewer would, and sit across from him or her, doing something moderately complicated such as math problems. Have your friend say at some point, "Stop. How much time has passed since we started?" Without looking at a watch, guess. Do this a few times until you get a good feel for how much time has passed.

If you're curious about how much time you can get away with, consider getting my Look Over My Shoulder program, which comprises audio recordings of approximately 20 case interviews I gave to real candidates. The program lets you listen in on these interviews and hear how different candidates handled each case. One of the conscious choices I made in editing these recordings was leaving the awkward moments of silences intact so you can hear for yourself just how long one or two minutes feels like from the interviewer's perspective.

In addition, the recordings include interviews with both strong and weak candidates, and during each recording I provide voiceover commentary, pointing out what the candidate did well or poorly, as he or she did it.

To learn more about the Look Over My Shoulder program, visit www.caseinterview.com/jump/loms.

Step #4: State Your Hypothesis

Let's say the client asks, "Should I shut down four of my factories and lay off 1,000 employees?" If you have sufficient information to state a well-informed hypothesis by now, you might say, "My initial working hypothesis is yes, you should shut down the factories. To test this hypothesis, I want to ..." This leads into step 5, structuring your case.

But if you don't have enough information to make a well-informed hypothesis, I recommend that you state an arbitrary hypothesis just to organize your analysis. Be sure to tell the interviewer it's an arbitrary hypothesis.

Let's say the interviewer says, "The client's profits have declined by 20 percent. What should the client do?" You might say, "Given the limited information we have to start, I'm going to state an *arbitrary* hypothesis that the client should cut costs to improve profits. This arbitrary hypothesis will help me organize my analysis, and I will quite likely revise my hypothesis as I discover more information. To test this hypothesis ..."

Deciding when to state your hypothesis is a point of contention among case interview experts and interviewers. Some argue that you just don't know enough information at the beginning of a case to make a well-informed hypothesis;

others argue that it's irrelevant if the hypothesis is actually true, because it's just something to force you to organize your problem-solving structure (step 5).

As a candidate, I was in the first school of thought, but having been a case interviewer and having coached many people through the process, I've come to realize that if a candidate does not state a hypothesis up front during a case interview, quite often he forgets to state a hypothesis at all during the case.

It may seem awkward to state a hypothesis when you have virtually no information, but this isn't a bad thing. If you state a ridiculous hypothesis to open a case, you'll feel enormous pressure to revise that hypothesis based on data you discover early in the case. And this is a *good* thing. If you don't state a hypothesis at the opening of a case, you're under no pressure even to form a hypothesis.

You don't have to state your hypothesis early in the opening of the case, but I suggest that you do. This approach works for more people more of the time than does the more sophisticated approach of delaying the hypothesis, which puts you at risk of forgetting to state a hypothesis at all.

Step #5: Decide, Draw, and Communicate Your Case Structure

The last step in opening a case is to structure your case for analysis. This involves identifying either a framework or a custom issue tree that will effectively test your hypothesis.

If your hypothesis is "The client should cut costs to turn around profits," ask yourself, "What *must* be true if cutting costs to turn around profits is the right decision?"

You might think, "Well, if costs recently increased dramatically while revenues remained constant, it makes sense to find a way to cut costs." And this is *exactly* how you want to think, because you can easily validate or disprove this type of statement by asking for some data. (This step, analysis, is the focus of the next chapter.)

You might then think, *Hey, wait a minute. The profitability framework covers both costs and revenues. I can use it to validate or disprove my initial hypothesis very quickly. OK, that's what I'll do.*

Once you decide on your case structure, draw it on a piece of paper, turn the paper 180 degrees to show the interviewer what you've drawn and written, and explain your structure and how it will test your hypothesis.

You might say, "If costs have recently skyrocketed, this measure seems to support my hypothesis of cutting costs as the primary way to improve profitability. If costs have remained unchanged in the past several years and revenues have declined, however, this measure suggests that some external factor triggered the initial decline in profit, so cutting costs might help, but it probably won't address the underlying problem very well."

Don't skip this step of explaining your structure and the rationale behind it. In a case interview, you need to justify *why* you're doing whatever you're doing.

You want to turn your diagram around not only to show the interviewer your work but also because that's exactly what your interviewer (who is most likely a working consultant when she isn't busy interviewing candidates) was doing with clients the day before interviewing you.

Guess what tends to happen when you act like a consultant, sound like a consultant, draw like a consultant, and analyze like a consultant? You get job offers so you can actually *be* a consultant. You *really* set yourself apart from other candidates when you act like a working consultant during the case interview.

Consultants draw diagrams to outline their problem-solving approach on a piece of paper, turn the paper around, and explain their rationale to clients because it *involves* clients in the problem-solving process. One of the easiest ways to get clients to accept the engagement team's final recommendation is to involve them every step of the way so they feel as though they've contributed to developing the final recommendation.

The next step in the candidate-led case interview process is to analyze the case structure you just set up, which the next chapter covers.

Chapter 18

HOW TO ANALYZE A CANDIDATE-LED CASE

IT'S MUCH EASIER to analyze a case you've framed correctly than one you haven't. By this point, you've stated your initial hypothesis, which almost certainly you'll change; laid out in a framework or an issue tree the key issues you need to analyze in order to test your hypothesis; and explained why your problem-solving structure would effectively test the hypothesis. The next step is to analyze the key issues in your framework or issue tree.

For our purposes, *analysis* is defined as *breaking apart something into its component pieces*. Consultants use phrases like *"disaggregate* the problem," *"break the problem down* into pieces," and *"segment* the problem into its component pieces" to refer to analysis. Think of your client's business as a bunch of Lego blocks, and during analysis you pull the blocks apart and examine each one individually.

The Value of Segmenting a Number or Problem

Let's say you live in a neighborhood with 100 residents, and one of the residents wins a $100 million lottery prize. *On average,* everyone in the neighborhood is now a millionaire. Based on population data, your neighborhood has become a millionaire's neighborhood, so the government has decided to impose on your neighborhood a "millionaire's" income tax rate of 80 percent. After all, *on average,* everyone in the neighborhood is a millionaire, right?

The consultant in you should be screaming, "Wait, that's misleading! You can't take 80 percent of my income in taxes!" We have to break apart the *average* and look at what it comprises. If you look carefully, just one lucky guy has $100 million — the other 99 residents aren't wealthy. Notice how this distinction paints an entirely different picture than "the average resident is a millionaire."

Why Totals and Averages Always "Lie"

Remember these two things:

- Total numbers "lie."
- Averages "lie."

Perhaps *lie* is too strong a word, but it's sure easy to remember. A more accurate term would be *mislead*. Anytime you hear a total number or an average number, assume it's a lie you need to segment or disaggregate to understand fully. Here are some examples of "lies":

- Total profits are $100 million.
- The average age of Facebook users is 25 years.
- The average loss on orders is $100.
- The average order size is $500.
- Our average customer service rating is 6 out of 10 points.
- Harvard's average acceptance rate is 8 percent.

Each of these "lies" should make you think, *We need to segment these numbers into their component pieces in order to grasp what's really going on.* So let's do that:

- Maybe the Eastern division made $1 billion in profits and the Western division lost $900 million, resulting in total profits of $100 million.
- Maybe 1 percent of Facebook users are more than 80 years old, but this is "buried" within the statement "The average age of Facebook users is 25 years."
- Maybe 10 percent of orders are extremely profitable, but 90 percent of orders aren't, resulting in an average loss of $100 per order.
- Maybe 1 percent of orders are more than $1 million, but 99 percent of orders are only $10, resulting in an average order size of $500.
- Maybe our average customer service rating with corporate accounts is 10 out of 10, but our average

customer service rating with small businesses is 1 out of 10, resulting in an overall average of 6 out of 10 points.

- Maybe children of Harvard alumni are accepted 40 percent of the time and everyone else is accepted 2 percent of the time, resulting in an average acceptance rate of 8 percent.

Notice how different these statements are from those above. They demonstrate *numerical* disaggregation—identification of the subcomponents that make up the total number. Consultants analyze data this way all day, every day, in order to give clients the insights they're looking for.

You can perform disaggregation qualitatively as well. For example, if your hypothesis is that the client should enter XYZ market, then you'll likely need to examine the customers. To validate the hypothesis, one of the branches of your problem-solving structure should say something along the lines of "Customer trends and composition are extremely attractive," which is a qualitative statement.

Exactly what makes the trends and composition "attractive"? In other words, what component pieces compose an attractive customer group? You could break this down into the number of customers versus each customer's likelihood to spend, so you define the "attractive" components as the large and growing number of customers, customers' strong desire individually to buy what the client sells, and customers' frustration with the lack of products that meet their needs.

This argument breaks down the meaning of *attractive* to explain in an easy-to-understand way which aspects of trends and composition are desirable in a customer group.

Let's consider another example. A friend tells you, "I think I'm in love. She'll be the perfect spouse. Should I marry her?"

That's a pretty unstructured question. How do you structure this kind of a decision? In other words, how do you disaggregate the concept of a "perfect spouse"? Maybe that determination is based on a certain set of benefits the potential spouse offers:

- o Emotional benefits (e.g., when life gets tough, she supports me)
- o Social benefits (e.g., she runs in social circles I'd like to run in)
- o Physical benefits (e.g., she's really attractive)
- o Financial benefits (e.g., her career's skyrocketing)

Notice my attempt to break down this analysis as much as possible to make it MECE (mutually exclusive, collectively exhaustive). It's nowhere near perfect, but it's certainly better than listing a dozen traits that potentially make an ideal spouse. Even a simple effort at MECE categorization can make your structure easier to follow.

Going back to our example, maybe you'd argue that the benefits shouldn't be weighted equally. Maybe you feel that emotional benefits represent 100 percent of the decision, and the other types of benefits represent 0 percent. That's a completely valid argument, but note that laying out the components (benefits) of a "perfect spouse" allows you to shape a more constructive and concrete discussion about what's important.

I've shared these examples to reinforce the idea that you can break down *anything* into its quantitative or qualitative component parts. And most consultants can't help but disaggregate everything.

When one of my female McKinsey colleagues was busy planning her wedding, she segmented her list of invited guests by the closeness of their relationship to her, their likelihood of attending, and whether they'd bring a guest. As people RSVP'd, my colleague updated the precision of her assumptions to predict head count more accurately. She used her data to create a financial forecasting model for the number of meals to order, the size of the cake to order, the square footage of dance floor needed, and multiple other variables.

Those of us who saw all her work reacted in one of two ways: "That's ridiculous!" or "That's so impressive!" We all started laughing, so the bride asked us, "Well, do you have a better idea?" And that shut us up, because we realized she was right. Someone in the group even asked, "Hey, after you get married, can I get a copy of your Excel model?"

The Analysis Process, Step-by-Step

Step #1: Phrase Each Qualitative Branch as a Sub-hypothesis

It's much easier to work with a framework or an issue you've broken down into component parts than with one you haven't. For example, in the profitability framework, we know the mathematical formula for profits is revenues minus expenses. It's easy to see in this quantitative situation that you need data on revenues and expenses to disaggregate profits.

Qualitative data such as customer analysis, however, needs to be rephrased before you can disaggregate it. Instead of saying "Customer analysis," say "Customers in this segment are extremely attractive," which changes your customer analysis from a passive exercise to an active one that you've designed to validate (or disprove) a specific point. This kind of subtle rephrasing makes it easier for most candidates to stay focused. In this case, you don't want to analyze customers just because you're supposed to; you want to analyze customers to determine if they're an attractive-enough audience for your client to target. The slight rephrasing of the branch makes it easier to keep this objective in mind.

Step #2: Drill Down Each Branch by Asking for Data

Now comes the fun part (seriously!) of analyzing each branch. Consultants use phrases like "drill down" and "pull up" to refer to the way in which consultants work down one branch of a framework or an issue tree until reaching a natural conclusion or dead end and then go back to the top of the framework or issue tree in order to start working down a different branch.

As you drill down each branch of your issue tree or framework, ask the interviewer (or client) for data to test your hypothesis or subhypothesis. For example, let's say you're analyzing profitability. You start off by drilling down the cost side of the framework, only to determine that the client's fixed and variable costs haven't really changed despite declining profits. Your analysis of the cost branch of the issue tree reveals that the number of units sold has declined quite severely.

At this point, you've reached a dead end in your disaggregation process. You realize you need to determine *why* the number of units sold has declined and disaggregate that number to identify which units declined in volume. You've finished drilling down the cost branch, so you have to pull up before you can drill down the other component of profits: revenues.

You'll get accustomed to drilling down and pulling up because you'll use it over and over again in both interviews and on-the-job assignments.

You must break down conceptual and qualitative topics such as "Customers in this segment are attractive" and "An ideal spouse provides financial benefits" into subtopics. For example, your breakdown of "Customers in this segment are attractive" might look like this (though the exact subcomponents would be highly dependent on the hypothesis you're trying to test):

- Number of customers
- Growth rate of number of customers
- Average spending per customer
- Potential spending per customer
- Customer needs versus client's offerings

Your breakdown of "An ideal spouse provides financial benefits" might look like this:

- Current income
- Future income
- Current assets
- Future assets (e.g., inheritance)

Breaking down larger topics into subtopics allows you to move your analysis from the branch level to the sub-branch level. Once you're at the sub-branch level, you can ask both quantitative and qualitative questions.

Step #3: Use a Process of Elimination

As you drill down, work through each issue until you determine whether it's a major contributing factor to your subhypothesis. For example, if your subhypothesis is that your friend's potential spouse has current and future financial resources, you'll look at the following factors:

- Current income
- Future income
- Current assets
- Future assets (e.g., inheritance)

Let's say that as you analyze each item, you discover that your friend's potential spouse doesn't have any current income, doesn't have any future prospects for income, doesn't possess any assets with any value, and isn't likely to inherit any such assets in the future.

By process of elimination, you've determined that your friend's potential spouse doesn't offer much in terms of financial benefits to your friend. Such a determination doesn't mean this potential spouse isn't a good match for your friend, but it does mean that financial benefits are not one of the reasons your friend wants to marry this woman.

Similarly, if you were doing a customer analysis and discovered very few potential customers in the market, you wouldn't automatically determine that the client should ignore the market. You would, however, consider this one offsetting factor the client needs to contemplate in determining whether to target a particular customer audience.

Perhaps few customers are buying today, but the number of new customers doubles every 30 days. In this case, the fast growth rate might more than compensate for the relatively small current market size. By laying out the logic in this way, you make it very clear what risk factors the client needs to consider in accepting your recommendation, and you also determine what factors you need to watch carefully should the client proceed with your recommendation.

Step #4: Revise Your Hypothesis (as Needed)

As you discover more information, you need to ask yourself constantly how the newly discovered data affects your hypothesis. Does it support your hypothesis? If so, continue your analysis. Does the new data disprove your hypothesis? If so, what *revised* hypothesis does the data validate?

If you need to revise your hypothesis, start the entire case process over from step 5 of the opening process — structuring your issue tree or framework. Repeat these steps until you cannot revise your hypothesis further.

Step #5: Stop One Branch and Move to Another

My blog readers often ask me, "When should I stop working on a particular branch?" I have two answers to this question:

- When you've reached a logical dead end
- When you've discovered an "aha" insight that prompts you to revise your hypothesis

If you're analyzing costs and realize that the client doesn't have a cost problem, it's time to pull up from that branch and move on to the remaining branches.

Let's say a client's profits have declined by $10 million over a certain period. You find that costs have increased by only $1 million over the same period, leaving a $9 million decline in profits unexplained by costs. If your initial hypothesis was that the client's profit problem was caused primarily by a huge increase in costs, you'd discover this wasn't true, so you'd revise the hypothesis to say, "Though the client's costs have increased slightly, the bulk of the decline in profits is due to a dramatic decline in sales."

At this point, you'd also want to stop analysis of costs, because costs *aren't* the *primary* cause of the client's problem.

You've deduced logically what is *not* the problem, so by process of elimination, what remains (in this example, revenues) must be the problem.

In a candidate-led case, you're responsible for deciding when to drill down, when to pull up, and when to switch to a different branch. The interviewer may hint that it's time to move on, but you can't depend on this. It's up to you to decide when to shift the focus in your analysis.

Step #6: Finish the Last Branch

When there's nothing meaningful left to test, you're done with your analysis. Your hypothesis can't be disproved and thus becomes your conclusion.

Tips for Better Analysis

The next chapter covers how to close out a case properly, but first, here are some tips you can apply to make your analysis first-rate:

Tip #1: Don't Jump Around Arbitrarily

Once you've laid out your problem-solving structure (preferably with a first level that's MECE), systematically and linearly tackle each branch in a logical, sequential order. Don't jump illogically from one branch to another. You should switch branches for one of only two reasons: (1) You've hit a logical dead end; or (2) you've revised your hypothesis and the underlying issue tree needed to test it, and your current topic of analysis is no longer included in the revised issue tree.

Tip #2: Propose a Solution Only after You've Isolated and Defined the Problem

Until you clearly define the client's problem and definitively isolate and prove the source of that problem, don't propose a solution.

Let's say a client wants to know what to do about its declining sales. Rephrase the client's request in your mind: *The client's sales have declined. The client wants me to (1) determine why this has happened, and (2) suggest what to do about it.* While the second request is explicit, most often the first request is implicit. Despite this, you still must resolve the first issue of *why* the problem has occurred in order to provide the proper solution.

Once you've clarified the problem, use the process of elimination to isolate its source; only then should you propose a solution. I've heard weaker candidates say the client should "increase sales commissions," "partner with another company," or "do a big marketing campaign." Those are all just guesses about what the underlying cause of the problem could be. Increasing sales commissions could be a valid solution, but it presupposes the client's current sales commission has changed for the worse or is not keeping up with the market— suppositions that have been neither tested nor validated with data.

Because the candidate-led format is so flexible and places you in the driver's seat, you won't have the benefit of a more structured format in which the interviewer might compel you to define the problem as a necessary step before proposing a solution.

Tip #3: Don't Maintain Your Hypothesis When Data Disproves It

If you've uncovered data that disproves your hypothesis, your hypothesis is wrong. Don't take it personally. Don't get emotionally wedded to your hypothesis. Don't deny the truth and try desperately to validate your hypothesis despite all the contrary facts, because you'll look terribly illogical.

It's OK—and expected—that you wonder aloud about what's going on in the case. You'll likely need to revise your hypothesis, and it's perfectly fine to say, "Clearly, my hypothesis isn't correct, and I'm not sure what is correct, so let me think about it." This lets the interviewer know you've used the process-of-elimination technique effectively, even if you're struggling to figure out what's left that must be true.

Tip #4: Show Your Issue Tree to the Interviewer

As you work through each branch of your issue tree, show your diagram to the interviewer. When you reach a dead end on a branch, put an X next to it to indicate that, via process of elimination, you know that specific branch isn't the primary cause of the client's problem.

To see a copy of a handwritten issue tree drawn correctly, take a look at my Look Over My Shoulder program, which contains several scanned images of hand-drawn issue trees.

For more information on this program, visit www.caseinterview.com/jump/loms.

Tip #5: Compare Your Numbers to Something Else

Comparing your data to something else is useful for establishing context and meaning. *My two favorite and most commonly used comparisons are historical comparison and competitive comparison. Write that down. Tattoo it on your hand. Never* forget it.

Let's say a client's profit margins (defined as profits divided by revenues) are 15 percent, but you have no idea if this is good or bad for this particular industry. If you found out that profit margins were 30 percent a year ago, then you'd deduce that something happened to the client's company during the past year to cause this problem.

If you found out that competitors' profit margins were 30 percent a year ago and 15 percent today, then you'd deduce that the client isn't alone—it's facing an industry-wide problem. (In this situation, you'd focus on understanding customers and competitors first and possibly skip part or most of the company analysis.)

If you found out that competitors' profit margins were 30 percent a year ago and remain unchanged at 30 percent today, then you'd deduce that the client is facing a company-specific problem. (In this situation, you'd do a company analysis and compare it to your competitive analysis to figure out why this issue is affecting only your client and not its competitors.)

Notice how by asking just two simple questions you can efficiently shift the focus on your analysis dramatically. Those are two very good questions to remember to ask!

Tip #6: Remember to Segment and Choose Your Words Carefully

Aggregate numbers can be segmented into component pieces in many different ways, and knowing *how* to ask for segmented data can easily save five to ten minutes of your time.

If you know sales are, say, $100 million, you could segment this figure by any number of criteria, including geographical region, type of customer, sales channel, product line, new versus old customers, or size of customer segment. The possibilities are infinite. So how do you know which variable to use to segment the data? The reality is, you don't (nor are you supposed to know). But the interviewer does.

You can ask for segmented data in such a way that the interviewer reveals to you the preferred segmentation pattern. Instead of saying, "I'd like to break down the $100 million in sales by geography," say, "I'd like to better *understand the sources of revenue that make up* the $100 million."

Notice how the second version doesn't specify that I want to segment by product line or geography. All I say is that I want to segment the data, period, and then I shut my mouth. You'll be tempted to talk, but don't do it. Just make your request and then stop talking. (It doesn't hurt to smile a little while waiting patiently for the interviewer to tell you the right answer.)

Most interviewers are happy to tell you, because they're evaluating whether you realized that a number needed to be segmented. The actual segmentation pattern a consultant uses in a client engagement is a function of trial and error, so you don't need to provide it, and no one will expect it (unless the background you've been given on the case implies a particular segmentation approach).

Case Interview Analysis Examples

The following example dialogues illustrate various aspects of the analysis phase of the case interview.

Example Dialogue #1: Drill-Down Analysis and Hypothesis Revision

Let's say we're tackling a profitability case. I like to use the profitability case structure for teaching purposes because it illustrates the process as cleanly as possible:

Interviewer: The client's profits are down $20 million, so the executive team needs your help to rectify the problem.

(Rephrase the situation in your head. What is the interviewer really asking you to do? Figure out why profits are down, and only after you've done this, tell the client how to fix the problem.)

Candidate: Let's start with an arbitrary initial hypothesis that profits are down $20 million because costs have increased out of control. To test this, I'd like to break down profits into its component parts: revenues and costs. How have these two numbers changed during this time period?

Interviewer: Revenues actually have decreased.

Candidate: Oh, interesting, OK.

(Data says that revenues have gone down, so revenue is likely the problem.)

Candidate: How much have revenues gone down by?

Interviewer: They've gone down by $20 million, actually.

Candidate: Revenues minus costs equals profits, and because both profits and revenues have declined by $20 million, costs have remained unchanged mathematically. My initial hypothesis that the client has a cost problem is incorrect. I'm going to revise my hypothesis to say that the decline in revenue is due to a drop in pricing. To test this hypothesis, I want to disaggregate revenues into its component parts: average selling price per item and number of items sold. Do we have any information on whether the number of units sold has changed? If so, has that number gone up, gone down, or stayed the same?

Interviewer: The number of units sold hasn't changed. We sold a million units last year and another million this year.

Candidate: Interesting. So profits have declined by $20 million, revenues have declined by $20 million, and units sold remains steady at a million. This implies that prices have declined by $20 per unit. Do we have any information on whether that's true?

Interviewer: Yes, prices are down by $20 per unit.

Candidate: OK, great. So the real underlying issue is that prices have declined, for some reason, by $20 per unit, and this is driving both sales and profits down by 20 percent.

(And then you just keep drilling down with a series of questions: Can we segment this $20 average price decline into its component parts? Can we see pricing changes for various products? Have prices for all products declined, or just for one? For products whose prices have declined, what percentage of unit sales does this represent? How does this compare to our competitors?)

Example Dialogue #2: The Dead End

Now let's look at what happens when you run into a dead end, using a different scenario from the case above.

Candidate: My hypothesis is that revenues have declined, which is why profits have dropped by $20 million. Do we have any information on whether revenues have changed?

Interviewer: In fact, revenues have increased by $20 million.

Candidate: Oh, that's interesting. Revenues have increased by $20 million, yet profits have *dropped* by $20 million.

(The revenue hypothesis is a dead end.)

Candidate: It must not be a revenue problem, so let's focus on costs next. This means costs have gone up by $40 million.

Interviewer: Yes, that's correct.

Candidate: OK, so my hypothesis is that one type of cost has gone up quite dramatically. My goal is to figure out which cost accounts for the bulk of the cost increase. To test this hypothesis, I'd like to break down cost into its component parts.

To start, I'd like to look at fixed versus variable costs. How have these two types of costs changed?

Interviewer: Fixed costs remain unchanged, and variable costs have increased.

Candidate: I'd like to segment variable costs into its components as well. Do we have more details on this?

Interviewer: Yes, we know that the number of units sold this year has remained the same.

Candidate: I see. That's really interesting. It suggests that the costs per unit have increased quite dramatically

Interviewer: Yes, that's correct.

Candidate: On a side note, this also suggests that the client must have had a price increase, because revenues have gone up but the number of units sold has remained unchanged. Is that right?

Interviewer: Yes.

Candidate: Despite the price increase, however, costs per unit appear to have increased faster than prices have.

Interviewer: Yes, that's correct as well.

Candidate: OK, I'd like to revise my hypothesis even further. Some costs—more specifically, one or more variable costs—have increased past the point where they could be offset by price increases. To test this, I'd like to understand what items make up the variable costs and how each item has changed.

Conclusion

These examples illustrate the cycle of drilling down, running into logical dead ends, and pulling up. With each dead end, we have to revise the hypothesis, adjust the issue tree structure to reflect the revised hypothesis, drill down again … lather, rinse, repeat.

At some point, one of two things will happen: (1) You'll run out of time and the interviewer will end the interview, or (2) you'll find and prove a hypothesis.

If you run out of time, the interviewer will say, "OK, we're about out of time. What would you recommend to the client?" or, "OK, let's say the client walks into the room and wants to know what you've learned."

If you have a hypothesis you can't disprove despite a solid issue tree structure and extensive analysis of each branch of the issue tree, you've reached a conclusion point in your case.

Either way, it's time to close the case.

Chapter 19

HOW TO CLOSE A CANDIDATE-LED CASE

CLOSING A CASE is about synthesis. If analysis is akin to pulling all the Lego blocks apart to evaluate each one individually, then synthesis is akin to reassembling all the blocks and telling the client, "Hey, it looks like a house! Here's why ..."

When you close a case, state the big picture first: "When we assemble all the Legos, they look like a house." State your conclusion *first* and then your supporting data points. Closing a case this way separates the stellar candidates from the typical ones.

Like music, a well-synthesized case has a certain rhythm and cadence. The following three examples of synthesis differ in their quality and rhythm:

- Poor — A poor close goes like this: Data data data data data data data data data ... part of the conclusion ... data data ... another part of the conclusion ... data data data ... another part of the conclusion.

  (*All the elements of this poor synthesis run into each other. It lacks structure, and it's hard to tell where the beginning, middle, and end are.*)

- Good — A good close goes like this: Conclusion, three relevant pieces of data that directly support that conclusion.

  (*This synthesis is OK but not stellar.*)

- Great — A great close goes like this: Conclusion with a definitive action recommendation, three pieces of data that are logically related to the conclusion, restatement of the conclusion.

  (*This synthesis is great because it restates the action-oriented recommendation, and the logic throughout is clear and toned.*)

Below is a nonbusiness example to illustrate the differences among poor, good, and great syntheses. The example below relates to communication with children—something near and dear to my heart because I have three daughters.

Let's say I go out one evening to run a few errands while I leave the kids with the babysitter. Like most kids, my kids always seem to find some way to get themselves in trouble. Upon my return, I try to find out what happened in my absence. In doing so, I get a different synthesis from each person involved:

- Poor synthesis—My middle daughter comes running to me and says, "Daddy! Daddy! Daddy! I'm sorry, it was an accident, but my sister made me do it. We weren't trying to. It was an accident. Not my fault, her fault. I know, candles—bad idea. Matches—I know. But she pushed me. She did, really. Oh, I'm coughing a lot! Help! What should I do?"

  (This synthesis is poor because it provides no insight as to what the hell is going on. There's a lot of information but no insight, conclusion, or action recommendation.)

- Better synthesis—My oldest daughter comes to me and says, "Dad, the house is on fire! We were playing with matches; let's get the hell out of here!"

  (That's an action-driven conclusion, right? You know exactly what the recommended course of action is, and you have a pretty good idea of the rationale.)

- Best synthesis—The babysitter comes downstairs. She's learning to become a management consultant, so she pulls out a PowerPoint presentation:

Action-oriented conclusion statement: "Mr. Cheng, the house is on fire; get out of the house now!"

- Slide 1: "The fire will consume the house in less than one minute. I've measured the width of the house to be 120 feet. The fire is moving 10 feet every five seconds. We have less than 60 seconds to live." *(Notice her use of quantitative data.)*

- Slide 2: "Putting out the fire is no longer possible. The fire's too damned big, not to mention that the fire extinguisher is at the opposite end of the house. And guess what, Mr. Cheng? I've been watching you work out, and you're not quite as fast as you used to be on the treadmill, so you won't make it."

- Slide 3: "You promised your wife you'd take care of the kids and the house while she was out. Well, one out of two ain't bad, provided you get out now to save the kids while you still can!"

Restated action-oriented conclusion statement: "As you can see, the only logical option is to get the hell out of the house with your kids right now!"

Obviously, this example is an attempt to be humorous, but it's also technically correct. Notice the structure of the communication:

Conclusion

- Supporting data #1
- Supporting data #2
- Supporting data #3

Restate conclusion

You could use this structure to convince a CEO to sell off a division of a company:

Ms. CEO, we recommend that you sell off the South American division of XYZ Corp.

- The division has lost money ten years in a row.
- Its two key competitors are ten times larger and have an estimated 15 percent cost savings advantage that XYZ Corp. cannot match.
- The largest customer segments are extremely price-sensitive, and the remaining segments are too small to make a difference.

For these reasons, we recommend selling off the South American division.

Get used to this structure. Practice it in everyday life. If a friend asks, "Where do you want to go to dinner?" start with a conclusion first. State three supporting data points. Restate the conclusion.

***

It is possible to get to the final round of interviews without great synthesis, but it's hard to get a final-round offer without it. The differences between merely adequate synthesis and truly exceptional synthesis are subtle.

For example, in my Look Over My Shoulder program, I interviewed one candidate who currently works for a top 15 consulting firm. She got to the final round at McKinsey but did not pass it. Before I discovered this about her background, I had given her a practice case interview and rated her performance a B+. At this level, I felt her performance was strong enough to work in the industry but not good enough to get an offer from the top three firms. My independent assessment of her performance ended up being precisely in alignment with McKinsey's assessment.

The three or four small things that made her performance a B+ instead of an A required very small adjustments—well within her ability to change once she was aware of what she was doing wrong.

You can listen to this interview recording along with my commentary (not to mention 20+ other interviews with similar analysis from the interviewer's perspective) in my Look Over My Shoulder program. More information is available at www.caseinterview.com/jump/loms.

PART SIX

Variations on the Candidate-Led Case

Chapter 20

THE INTERVIEWER-LED CASE

THE INTERVIEWER-LED CASE, sometimes called the "command and control"-style case, features a highly structured format that typically consists of five discrete phases. The interviewer dictates the focus, tempo, and sequence of your problem solving.

McKinsey has moved exclusively to this format in recent years (and so far is the only firm to have done so). Concomitantly, it started requiring that its interviewers use cases from a central collection rather than make up their own. To understand the implications of these shifts, you need to understand the history behind case interviews at McKinsey and in the rest of the industry.

For many years, the traditional candidate-led case format was the de facto standard in the consulting industry, and each interviewer created his or her own cases, often inspired by client work. As a result, cases varied tremendously from interviewer to interviewer. Under these circumstances, to succeed in this interview format, candidates had to excel at both structuring an enormously wide range of problems and managing the overall problem-solving process, as well as demonstrate and seamlessly *integrate* all four problem-solving tools: hypothesis, issue tree, analysis, and synthesis.

Two important changes occurred when McKinsey shifted to using centrally standardized, interviewer-led cases, which essentially have made the case interview easier for candidates. First, you no longer need to integrate all four problem-solving tools. Because the interviewer leads the case, he integrates these skills for you in some ways. Second, because interviewer-led cases contain little ambiguity, the analysis portion of the case is much easier. What used to require an extensive process-of-elimination analysis has largely been replaced by a less difficult math problem that more candidates can solve. As a result, stellar analysis no longer differentiates one candidate from another—at least not to the degree it used to.

Now you have to differentiate yourself with only three of the four tools: hypothesis, issue tree, and synthesis. Candidates can give a variety of acceptable hypotheses for a case, so this portion of the case also doesn't differentiate one candidate from another.

Your performance in this type of case depends disproportionately on your use of just two of the key problem-solving tools: issue tree and synthesis. So don't screw up on these two pieces, because you can't make up for it with the other two tools.

Now let's look at the format and how to perform well in it. We need to review our four core problem-solving tools—yes, all four, because they still apply to interviewer-led cases. But because the interviewer leads the case, its dynamic and tempo—its overall structure—will feel quite different, especially if you don't anticipate the sudden change in style.

Case Format Structure

Unlike in a candidate-led case, the transition from hypothesis to issue tree to analysis to synthesis can be quite abrupt in an interview-led case. If you take an unusually long time on one of these areas, the interviewer may politely cut you off and shift to the next phase of the case.

If this happens to you, don't take offense; it's actually to your advantage. If you don't get the chance to perform each step of the case, you'll get rejected automatically. But if the interviewer cuts you off at a particular point in the case because you haven't yet reached a natural transition point, you're probably moving too slowly and being inefficient in your approach.

The primary problem-solving tools used in the interview-led case mirror those used in the candidate-led case: hypothesis, issue tree, analysis, and synthesis (skewed toward issue tree and synthesis, which are the areas where candidates' performance varies the most).

The following outline illustrates the typical structure of an interviewer-led case:

1. Introduction/hypothesis—The interviewer explains the client's major problem and asks you for your hypothesis.

2. Problem structuring/issue tree—The interviewer asks you how you would structure this problem. More explicitly, the interviewer wants to know how you would break down this problem into its component parts in a way that would allow you to test the hypothesis.

3. Analysis—The interviewer jumps to a particular issue in the case and asks you to perform some type of quantitative analysis.

4. Business acumen/brainstorming question—The interviewer asks you to brainstorm numerous potential solutions to one aspect of the client's problem. The twist is that you're supposed to come up with ideas only, not analyze them. This step sometimes appears early in the case, but more commonly it appears later.

5. Synthesis—The interviewer asks you to close the case.

The flow of the outline above is based on McKinsey's interview format as of the time I wrote this book. McKinsey and other firms may change the format's sequencing or time allocation, or perhaps insert or remove steps, so don't get too accustomed to this particular five-step model. Instead, get accustomed to the dynamic of the interviewer leading the case and to the modular aspects of the case.

Subtle Aspects of the Interviewer-Led Case

Because of this case format's modularity, you have to manage your time differently than you do in other case formats. Unlike in a candidate-led case, once you finish a section of an interviewer-led case, it's over. So you need to be thorough at every phase of the case, because you won't be able to go back later in the case to "rescue" something you missed previously.

The rigidity of this format also necessitates that you finish each phase in five to ten minutes. Typically the interviewer will give you five minutes for each phase except the quantitative analysis, which sometimes takes longer.

Don't let the modularity of the case mislead you into thinking it's five independent mini-cases; it's still just one case. You need to link what you learn in each step of the case back to the client's original objective and your hypothesis. Be sure to approach the case at *both* the module level and the overall level.

Phases of the Case

Let's look at each of the five steps of this case format in greater detail.

Step #1: Introduction/Hypothesis

At the opening of the case, the interviewer will provide some background information on the client's situation and identify the client's primary problem, question, or objective. In this phase, you'll want to establish a hypothesis you can test and refer to throughout the rest of the case. One of a number of different scenarios will happen next:

- The interviewer will flat out ask you, "What do you think is going on here? What's your best guess as to what the client should do?" (In other words, "What's your hypothesis?")

- The interviewer will give you the hypothesis she wants you to use. She might say, "The client thinks that X is the right decision." (In other words, "This is the hypothesis you're going to use.") The interviewer then might immediately segue into step 2: problem structuring/issue tree development.

- The interviewer will *imply* a hypothesis without asking for one from you. Sometimes the interviewer's description of a case's background implies a hypothesis—for example, "The client's sales are falling, so it is considering shutting down XYZ division." (Implied hypothesis: "The client should shut down XYZ division.")

- The interviewer will say that the client is considering one of three options—for example, "The client is considering shutting down the division, selling it off, or attempting to turn it around." If this happens, you can phrase your hypothesis in such a way as to incorporate testing the other options implicitly. For example, you might say, "For argument's sake, let's hypothesize that the client should turn around the business *because* it's more attractive than is shutting it down or selling it." The "because" in the sentence forces you to create an issue tree in step 2 to test the reason that follows "because."

Regardless of how the topic of a hypothesis comes up (or perhaps doesn't come up), you still need a hypothesis. You need to have one in mind, at the very least, going into step 2. Ideally, you verbally articulate your hypothesis, even if the interviewer doesn't prompt you for one. If the interviewer implies or gives you the hypothesis, verbally confirm your recognition of that by stating the hypothesis explicitly.

If you're not familiar with this case format, its brusqueness might throw you off. Some candidates have told me that the interviewer cut them off midsentence and "stole" the case by taking it over. Others have complained they didn't get to work with the hypothesis they wanted or were asked to analyze an issue that wasn't in their framework.

The interviewer is in charge of the case, which is why some people call it the "command and control" case format. This format doesn't actually feel as aggressive as it sounds here, but it could throw you off if you're not expecting it.

Step #2: Problem Structuring/Issue Tree Development

In this step, the interviewer asks you to create a problem-solving structure to test the hypothesis, whether it's yours, the client's, or the interviewer's. If the interviewer doesn't provide, suggest, imply, or ask you for a hypothesis, formulate one and state it while structuring the case in this step. Expect the interviewer to ask these or similar questions:

- How would you test your theory/hypothesis? What data would you need?
- How would you approach solving this problem?
- What are the *most important* factors to consider in developing a recommendation for the client?
- What *key issues* must you consider to answer the client's question?
- What *primary drivers* would you need to analyze for a problem such as this one?

Because of the modular aspect of this format, you'll need to make a major adjustment here if you're accustomed to the candidate-led case format. In the candidate-led case, you can use an issue tree with just a single level (e.g., profit equals revenues minus costs) as a starting point and then reveal the subsequent levels as you drill down over the course of the next 30 minutes of the case.

This interviewer-led case format doesn't permit you to drill down and expand the detail of your structure as you analyze. Instead, you have to outline the entire structure up front. You have only five minutes to identify *all the layers* of your issue tree structure *and* justify why each layer belongs in the structure *and* explain what you expect to learn from each layer.

(You could use this approach in candidate-led cases, but I never did. Then again, I interviewed during a much less competitive time, and candidates were far less prepared. If I were interviewing today, I would explain two or three layers of my issue tree in my opening, regardless of case format.)

Extremely high performers in case interviews routinely do a good job explaining why they're inclined to do certain things in a case's problem-solving structure. Average performers will recall a so-called standard framework and a few questions associated with it. These performers might then remember to ask the "standard" questions that go with the "standard" framework but won't actually think about and explain *why* a particular question is or isn't relevant to that particular case.

A good interviewer will challenge you and ask you *why* you're inclined to do certain things. A strong candidate will proactively and preemptively answer that question so the interviewer doesn't have to do anything more than nod in approval and be impressed.

My blog readers send me their success stories (www.caseinterview.com/success-stories) all the time. Some readers' opening structures have been so good that the McKinsey interviewer couldn't help but say, "Yes, that's an absolutely perfect structure. I totally agree. Please proceed." Not surprisingly, McKinsey offered these individuals jobs.

As I mentioned, because the interviewer-led case is much easier than the other formats are, the two primary places to differentiate your ability in this type of interview are in the problem structuring (create and justify a multilayered issue tree) and synthesis. It's important to master these two areas, which are the primary points of differentiation among candidates of differing skill levels.

Step #3: Analysis

As soon as you've defined the initial structure, the interviewer will jump to a particular issue for you to analyze. The interviewer will have picked the topic before the interview began, so it may not be related to your issue tree. If you set up your issue tree comprehensively, however, the topic should fall somewhere within it, either as a core branch or perhaps a sub-branch.

If the new topic doesn't fit into your structure anywhere, your structure might not be comprehensive enough (which is worth considering in your post-mortem analysis of your interview performance). Try not to get flustered if this happens, because it doesn't automatically mean your structure is poor. Sometimes the analysis will be on some side issue that the interviewer wouldn't necessarily expect to see in everyone's structure.

Typically, the interviewer will give you some type of prestructured quantitative analysis and a handout containing a bunch of data and then ask you a question that requires you to use the data on the handout to run some computations. Usually the computations consist of arithmetic (addition, subtraction, multiplication, division) and occasionally a single-variable algebraic equation (solve for X). The three most difficult parts of this analysis are the following:

- Translating a verbal question into the appropriate formulas
- Avoiding confusion caused by a multipart problem
- Avoiding careless errors due to stress

The actual math isn't difficult, but you have to figure out which math to use and when to use it, so this is where candidates unaccustomed to doing math, especially under pressure, make mistakes.

Sometimes the analysis involves a multicomponent math problem whose individual components usually aren't difficult to solve. But if you don't take good notes, you can easily get confused when you're trying to figure out the correct formula to use or in calculating the answer.

Let's look at an example of the type of math involved at this point in a case.

The client has three products: A, B, and C. The client doesn't change the price of product A; raises the price of product B by 15 percent, causing units sold to fall by 10 percent; and reduces the price of product C by 20 percent, causing unit sales to increase by 30 percent. How does the company's overall profit change, and by how much? Conceptually, the answer can be derived by the following formulas:

Sales change = new sales - old sales
New sales = sales A + sales B + sales C

Many candidates, including those with PhDs in physics or math, are extremely tempted not to write down these formulas. After all, it's obvious that the company's overall profit comprises the profits from all its products. So instead of writing out the formula for new sales, they immediately jump into a numerical equation. (The following data is fictitious, so the figures won't be realistic.)

$$\text{New sales} = \$1{,}000 + ((100 \times .9) \times (\$20 \times 1.15))$$
$$+ ((100 \times 1.3) \times (\$20 \times .8))$$

The problem with jumping straight to a numerical equation is that it's hard to double-check your numbers. You may be doing other math problems, and it's just too easy to transpose a number or flip an order of operations. If you don't write down the formula using words in place of actual numerical values, you may make a mistake, but you won't have anything against which to check your numerical equation. So here's how I do this kind of math:

Objective
Sales change = new sales - old sales
New sales = sales A + sales B + sales C

On a different piece of paper (or a different section of the paper), I write this:

Sales A = $1,000 (unchanged)

Then I go back to my original piece of paper and revise my formula:

New sales = sales A + sales B + sales C
New sales = $1,000 + sales B + sales C

Next I go back to my second piece of paper and compute another variable:

Sales B = quantity x price
Sales B = (100 units x .9) x ($20 x 1.15)
Sales B = 90 units x $23
(I'd do this computation on the side and double-check it)
Sales B = $2,070

Then I go back to my original piece of paper and revise the formula as follows:

New sales = sales A + sales B + sales C
New sales = $1,000 + sales B + sales C
New sales = $1,000 + $2,070 + sales C

Solving the entire problem systematically, one component at a time, vastly reduces the complexity of the math *and* how many numbers I need to memorize. This approach eliminates the need to remember *any* numbers, which is one of the secrets to avoiding confusion.

You're much less likely to make a careless error under stress if you break down the math into very simple problems. I gravitated toward the breakdown technique during a final-round interview at McKinsey. Unexpectedly, the interviewer asked me to do a math computation on a whiteboard. To make it easier for him to follow my thought process, I wrote out my formula in all words first. Then I solved each piece one at a time, adding each piece back into the formula one at a time, as shown above. I did this to make sure the interviewer followed my train of thought, and then I realized I could follow my own train of thought better this way too.

During my time at McKinsey, I found clients were intimidated if I did too much math in my head. They couldn't do the raw math as quickly as I could, and they certainly didn't want to admit to this. And clients who don't follow the math aren't likely to "buy in" to the results of the analysis. Because of this, I always use words in my formulas first and then do the math. This is a *big* secret to extremely high math accuracy in stressful case interviews.

Step #4: Business Acumen/Brainstorming Question

Usually sometime late in the case, the interviewer asks you to brainstorm a bunch of ideas for how to address the client's problem beyond what you've had time to analyze formally. At this point, keep in mind two things:

- The interviewer doesn't want you to set up an issue tree or prove or analyze anything. He simply wants to hear your ideas.

- Although this may feel like casual brainstorming, you don't have to do it in an unstructured, disorganized way.

Let's say you determine in the main portion of a case that the client profitability problem is a result of falling sales in one market segment—a segment in which the customers are aging and literally dying. Perhaps your quantitative analysis was able to prove this point.

The interviewer might then ask you, "What are all the different ways you can think of to help this client grow sales?" In a traditional brainstorming session, you might produce this laundry list:

- Raise prices
- Increase frequency of purchase
- Target a new customer segment
- Expand existing distribution channels to increase market share
- Adopt new distribution channels to increase market share
- Introduce new products
- Acquire a competitor

This list of ideas is just that—a list. It doesn't show the interviewer the two things she is looking for in order to evaluate your business acumen: (1) whether your ideas make sense, and (2) whether you can think broadly and comprehensively about the problem right after doing a super-detailed drill-down analysis. In a sense, the interviewer wants to verify that you can shift easily from supermicro- to supermacro-level thinking. If you provide a comprehensive list with reasonable ideas, you'll most likely pass this phase of the interview.

But you can answer this question in a better way, one that presents the answer in a more structured and organized fashion. Instead of making a laundry list of ideas, define the *categories* of your ideas and then list each category and its related ideas.

Let's use the question from above: "What are all the different ways you can think of to help this client grow sales?" I would say, "I can think of two categories of ideas. Let me define them and then give you the ideas I have in mind within each category."

Then I'd present the following categorization to the interviewer, explaining how each idea would help grow the client's sales:

- Grow sales in the existing customer segment
  o Raise prices
  o Increase frequency of purchase
  o Expand existing distribution channels to increase market share
  o Adopt new distribution channels to increase market share
  o Introduce new products
  o Acquire a competitor that focuses on this segment

- Grow sales in a new customer segment
  o Target a new customer segment and sell existing products
  o Use new products to target a new customer segment
  o Acquire a competitor that targets a new customer segment

This structured approach demonstrates much greater organization and clarity than does a laundry list. The structure also lends itself to categorization along MECE (mutually exclusive, collectively exhaustive) lines, which can help you be more thorough in generating ideas. For example, the brainstormed ideas contain three themes: new customer segments, new products, and new distribution (which, incidentally, is another categorization structure that would have worked). Let's systematically combine the three traits like this:

- New customer + new product + new distribution
- Old customer + new product + new distribution
- Old customer + old product + new distribution

We can then consider every possible combination to see which seems most logical and practical. You don't have to use a categorization structure or ensure that your list of ideas is MECE, but doing so could distinguish you from your competition.

In addition, it's important to realize that you're expected to be *conversational* in answering this question. So unlike with setting up a case's problem-solving structure out the outset, where it's permissible to take a minute or two to structure a case, during this more conversational interview structure you might stall a little and give yourself ten seconds to think on the fly before you answer the question.

Although this might seem extremely challenging, in practice the question is usually a relevant one where, in all likelihood, in working through the case you would have already considered some of the answers in your final response.

Step #5: Synthesis

The interviewer will ask you to finish up the case by synthesizing it. No matter how the interviewer phrases the question, do not merely summarize the case or recount every analysis you did. Instead, deliver your synthesis using the structure previously described:

Conclusion

- Supporting point 1
- Supporting point 2
- Supporting point 3

Restate conclusion

You could instead use a slightly more sophisticated structure:

Conclusion

- Supporting point 1
- Supporting point 2
- Supporting point 3

Restate conclusion *and* identify any unexplained issues *and* explain what you'd analyze next if you had more time

So instead of restating the conclusion by saying, "... and that's why I recommend the client shut down Factory 2," you'd say, "... and that's why I recommend the client shut down Factory 2. In addition, if we had more time, I'd want to further analyze the business's ability to be profitable in the long run with only Factories 1 and 3, to determine if the client should remain in this business in any capacity."

In the consulting business, the "if only we had more time" conclusion is how partners sell phase 2 of a project to a client. That one phrase is responsible for all the profit made in consulting. So when you close a case with an "if only we had more time" statement, the partner hears "ka-ching!" And that means more revenue. Partners will never admit this to you out loud, but the thought definitely crosses their mind. And because you've closed the case this way, they'll want to continue working with you because you've already made their life so much easier.

As I've said, consulting firms do specific things in the recruiting process quite deliberately. The better you understand how they think and why they think that way, the easier it'll be for you to give them what they want.

***

To hear audio samples of an interviewer-led case interview, take a look at the Look Over My Shoulder program, which consists of nearly ten hours of recordings from interviews with actual candidates. For more information, visit www.caseinterview.com/jump/loms.

Chapter 21

THE WRITTEN CASE INTERVIEW

IN THE TRADITIONAL candidate-led case interview, the candidate receives only the data she requests. She typically has a hypothesis in mind, knows what data is needed, and anticipates that the data will either support or refute the hypothesis. Because the interviewer doesn't ask the candidate to interpret data she did *not* ask for, the candidate-led case interview doesn't test the candidate's ability to sift through large quantities of data and determine what's important (or what's not)—a skill consulting firms in fact value.

Some firms use candidates' standardized test scores to assess this skill. Although the exact type of test score requested will vary by country, in the United States, firms ask for a candidate's SAT (college entrance exam), GMAT (business school entrance exam), or GRE (graduate school entrance exam) score or the score of some other standardized test for which percentile scores are available for objective comparison across a large population of test takers. The math portion of these exams often contains a section on data interpretation and numerical critical reasoning—the skills consulting firms seek. Most firms use a candidates overall math test score as a way to gauge these more specific skills.

Based on recent trends, however, I suspect these firms discovered that test scores alone are not a sufficiently accurate predictor of this skill. The data interpretation sections of standardized tests typically account for only 10 to 15 percent of the score, so it's possible for a candidate to score well on one of these exams but lack mastery of the crucial data interpretation skill that consulting firms value.

Consulting firms value this data interpretation skill so much that McKinsey uses a computer-based assessment called the McKinsey Problem Solving Test (PST) to screen out candidates even before the first case interview. This test consists of extensive data interpretation, numerical critical reasoning, and math speed and accuracy questions.

Bain has been experimenting with giving candidates two hours to analyze 45 pages of exhibits and then asking the candidates to take a one-hour exam that includes building a presentation based on the data in the exhibits. The Boston Consulting Group (BCG) has developed and is now using its own variation on McKinsey's PST to evaluate some of its candidates.

This background forms the basis for why many firms began using written assessments and cases during the recruiting process. Keep this context in mind when reading below about how to prepare for a written case.

I find the phrase "written case" a bit misleading because it suggests incorrectly that there's a single format called a *written case*. It's more accurate to think of a written case as a *component* that constitutes some percentage of a broader case or assessment.

For example, the candidate-led case is mainly a verbal case. The interviewer-led case used by McKinsey contains two to four pages that comprise several written exhibits and a data table, so we might say this type of case is 25 percent written. As noted, Bain candidates in Western Europe are given 45 pages of charts, exhibits, memos, articles, and data tables to analyze—meaning that 100 percent of the data provided is written—before taking a written test about the case and preparing a slide presentation using fill-in-the-blank templates.

Clearly, the written case covers a wide range of scenarios, including cases in which some or all of the background information (sometimes dozens of pages) is provided to the candidate in written form and others in which everything the candidate does during the interview is written down.

How to Prepare

In many respects, preparing for a written case is quite difficult. You can study and practice case methodology for many of the other formats (as I've described in this book) in an effort to improve your abilities, but data interpretation is a logical skill that some people find easy and others find extremely challenging. You can certainly improve your skill in this area, but I believe there's a cap on how much you can improve.

Some consulting firms like using the written format precisely because preparing for data interpretation tasks in candidate assessments and written cases is so hard. These firms often seek the candidates with the strongest raw intellectual talent. As the thinking goes, a firm can teach a highly intelligent consultant how to apply its methodology, but the firm can't teach someone who knows its methodology how to be highly intelligent.

To prepare for the written case, you need to assess how strong your math, logic, and data interpretation skills are. If you're typically very strong in math, then you likely possess this inherent raw talent. Focus on getting accustomed to tackling these kinds of questions and training your brain to be highly active and used regularly for math questions.

If math isn't your strength, as evidenced by standardized test scores, you have an interesting decision to make: Should you invest your time improving your data interpretation skills or practicing case interviews?

When it comes to data interpretation, the rate of return on your investment of time in terms of measurable improvement is fairly low. You may be able to improve your performance in this area by 10 to 25 percent but probably not by 50 percent or more. So if you're interviewing with a firm that doesn't rely much on written assessments or cases, then it's probably not worth putting in more than an hour or two of data interpretation practice.

In contrast, if you're interviewing with a firm that uses a lot of written assessments or cases and you know from your standardized test scores that data interpretation isn't your strength, then it's probably worth investing a considerable amount of time and effort to strengthen your skills in this area.

Preparation Resources for Written Data Interpretation and Exams

GMAT and GRE practice test books are the best resources for data interpretation practice. My website contains a list of practice test books I've personally evaluated whose sample questions require the use of skills that most closely resemble the type of data interpretation skill necessary to pass a written assessment (like the McKinsey PST) and the data interpretation portion of a written case. My website also contains some links to sample data interpretation questions and even a few practice exams. You can find all these resources in my online guide to the McKinsey PST at www.caseinterview.com/jump/pst.

Preparation Resources for Written Presentations

For guidance on preparing for written presentations, refer to Chapter 23, "The Presentation-Only Case Interview." The guidelines applicable to written cases and presentation-only cases overlap, so I've opted to cover the topic in just one place to avoid redundancy.

Written Assessments vs. Written Cases

In a data interpretation written *assessment*, the interviewer presents you with a bunch of exhibits and asks you very specific prestructured questions about them. Following is one example:

> Given Exhibit 3, which of the following statements is true? (1) Sales have grown at a compound annual growth rate exceeding 15 percent per year. (2) Sales have doubled in the past five years.

These questions tend to be formatted as "Can I assert X conclusion, given Y data?"

In a written *case*, you're expected to solve the case, not answer a set number of questions in an exam.

Sometimes the interviewer won't tell you whether you're getting an assessment or a case. So what should you do? Just ask: "Excuse me, but I'd like some clarification about the process. I know you'll be giving me a bunch of exhibits. Will you be asking me a set of predefined questions about the case, like in an exam, or will we engage in more of a problem-solving dialogue to figure out the case together?"

If the interviewer gives you a truly open-ended, ambiguous case, refer to your four core problem-solving tools: hypothesis, issue tree, analysis, and synthesis. If the interviewer asks a bunch of prestructured, extremely well-defined questions, you probably don't need the core problem-solving tools, because the assessment will involve logic, critical reasoning, and data interpretation.

Chapter 22

THE GROUP CASE INTERVIEW

AS THE NAME of the group case interview format suggests, you complete the case as part of a team consisting of other candidates. Yes, you'll be working *with* your "competition" (i.e., other candidates) to solve the case.

Monitor & Company uses this format in certain rounds of its interview process, and my blog readers tell me that McKinsey has experimented with this format in certain offices too.

Firms constantly experiment with and refine their recruiting processes to find the hidden talent in a large pool of applicants. They analyze promotion rates and firing rates of the people hired over the previous two years in order to assess the performance of their hiring process. They assess and analyze multiple topics, including whether your cohort performed as expected and what the poor performers had in common. Then they'll question the original recruiting process used to hire your cohort and analyze how it could have been improved to prevent future poor performers from making it into the organization.

Many of the changes in the case interview process come about because some consultants performed poorly on the job at some firm. Keep this in mind as I elaborate on why the group case format exists and what I think it is intended to uncover about a candidate. If you understand this underlying motivation, you'll immediately grasp how to perform well in this case format—even if you forget all the specific guidance I share later in this chapter.

Why New Consultants Fail

To understand the genesis of the group case interview format, it's useful to know *why* new consultants fail on the job—it's typically because they either have poor client management skills or refuse to acknowledge their errors.

Poor Client Management Skills

If a new consultant knows the analytically correct answer but the client disagrees (and is factually incorrect) for some reason, the consultant should *never* tell the client that she is dead wrong, especially in front of the client's direct reports, peers, or boss. In the consultant's eagerness to prove himself correct, he could embarrass, humiliate, and anger the client. The client will pin her anger on someone, so if you're the consultant who embarrassed the client, you're an easily expendable target. (Instead, the consultant should *diplomatically* express a "different perspective," explain his logic, and allow the client the opportunity to see things from this new perspective, without embarrassment.)

If the partners must choose between having a pissed-off client and removing you from the case team, guess what? You're off the team. In addition, news like this travels fast within an office, and no partner will want you on his or her team. You won't get staffed, or you'll become the last-choice consultant in the office.

Here's the key insight in this disaster scenario: Consultants who do something like this could pass the traditional case interview format with flying colors because they're never put in a situation in which they need to tell clients they're wrong.

Being Stubborn and Argumentative

Some new consultants have a hard time accepting ideas they didn't come up with first. If a new consultant were to think for some unfounded reason that the right approach is X and someone else on the team has the hard data to back up another approach, Y, the teammate clearly would be right. Some consultants have a very hard time accepting they're wrong, so to save face they push hard for what they know is a wrong position. Instead, they should accept that someone else is right, acknowledge it, and agree to proceed with the other person's plan or idea.

Engagement managers don't want consultants on their teams who are stubborn, inflexible, and argumentative. In consulting, insights (especially counterintuitive ones) backed by facts rule the day. What you think doesn't matter unless you can support and prove it with facts. If the facts are on your side, you're expected to present your perspective. If they're not, you need to be flexible enough to see that and move on. In other words, don't be adversarial.

Because the traditional case interview format doesn't position the candidate to be told he is wrong, the interviewer can't possibly predict how the candidate would react to being refuted. Would the candidate take a comment personally and be defensive, or would he realize that someone else is correct and accept it gracefully?

The group case format allows interviewers to observe how the candidate acts under pressure and reacts to being in a potentially argumentative environment.

The "Enemy" Is the Case, Not Your Teammates

Think of the other candidates in your group case as your teammates—you're working together, not competing against each other, to solve the client's problem.

So if one of the other candidates says something really stupid, don't yell out, "Hey, you're a moron. That's totally wrong. You should get rejected!" You want to resist that temptation for two reasons: (1) Assuming your sentiment is accurate, the interviewers already know if someone is saying something dumb, and it's not your job to tell them; and (2) belting out such insults reflects poorly on your potential client management skills.

As mentioned, consultants must possess good client management skills. Clients (especially more junior clients) will *routinely* express their opinions about a company's direction, but they can't support their opinions with any facts. A consultant with good client management skills can find a diplomatic way to tell clients they're wrong or—better yet—provide the information that will let the clients discover for themselves they're wrong.

I've been told I'm extremely good at telling clients they're totally wrong. In reality, I don't *tell* clients they're wrong. Instead, I speak with them face-to-face, ask questions, and introduce facts that I know will lead them to an inevitable conclusion. Rather than assert the conclusion for a decision I know will be controversial, I lead clients to the decision. I rarely take this tack in a written communication, in which I typically start with the conclusion. But in a group meeting that's consensus-building–oriented, I will lead in this way to avoid making anyone look bad in front of his or her peers.

One of the specific objectives of the group case format is to assess how diplomatically you tell your co-interviewees that you disagree with them. Interviewers also will assess how you handle co-interviewees who have *good* ideas. If someone else comes up with a good idea or extends your idea, you *must* acknowledge it and work with it. Give credit where credit is due instead of shooting down an idea because you want another candidate to look bad.

If someone adds to your idea, you can certainly do the same with the new version of the idea. This happens all the time in actual team meetings, when it's quite common for Consultant A to come up with the hypothesis, Consultant B to think of a good issue tree structure to test, and Consultant C to find a better way to test the hypothesis with a simpler issue tree. This continual refinement of thinking is *precisely* what consulting firms seek in their consultants, and the group case format does an excellent job creating circumstances in which this can happen and be evaluated.

In real life, I wouldn't want to be on a team with a consultant who's going to shoot down my ideas constantly. I actually like working with someone who spots flaws in my thinking but *doesn't* shoot me down personally, *does* incorporate my ideas into his or her own, and *does* add some insight or fact to make my original idea better.

Remember, it's NOT you versus the other interviewees. It's you and the other interviewees versus the case. Solve the case, work with your co-interviewers to solve the case, and—as we learned in Chapter 6—whatever you do, *don't be an asshole.*

The group case problem-solving process is similar to the traditional case interview process: hypothesis, issue tree, process-of-elimination analysis, synthesis. Firms often combine the group case format with elements of the written case interview format, so you should be familiar with both formats in case you encounter a hybrid of the two.

Chapter 23

THE PRESENTATION-ONLY
CASE INTERVIEW

IN A TRADITIONAL candidate-led case interview, the interviewer observes you using four tools to solve a problem: hypothesis, issue tree, analysis, and synthesis.

In a presentation-only case interview, you're given one or two hours by yourself to sift through charts and other types of data, develop a hypothesis, structure your issue tree, and analyze your findings. You then synthesize your findings in a slideshow presentation to the interviewer.

At the time of this writing, BCG and Bain offices in certain countries are testing whether this format, which emphasizes results rather than process, is a true indicator of a candidate's skills. Those firms are studying whether they can forget about assessing a candidate's hypothesis, issue trees and frameworks, and analysis skills and instead assess the end product for a solid structure and factual support. These firms reason that it's nearly impossible to create a well-synthesized presentation without executing all the other steps effectively.

You'll likely be disappointed if you expect that the interviewer will sit back and passively listen to your presentation. He will challenge every word you've said and every assertion or conclusion you've made. In essence, he wants to know if you can back up your words with rigorous analysis or if you're presenting just a bunch of words.

Tackling this case format effectively requires that you know how to do three things:

1. Process the big stack of printed charts and data the interviewer gives you (refer to Chapter 21, "The Written Case Interview," for information on how to do this)
2. Create a synthesis-oriented presentation
3. Present your findings

You have the foundation skills to create a presentation and present it verbally already. Instead of worrying about the word *presentation*, think of the task at hand as synthesis communicated via slides.

Structure of a Slide Presentation

A synthesis-oriented slide presentation has the exact same structure as a verbally presented synthesis:

Conclusion

- Supporting point 1
- Supporting point 2
- Supporting point 3

Restate conclusion

Presentation Structure Based on Length

Each firm has its own expectations about how long your presentation should be. If a firm gives you a lot of time to prepare and present, then it makes sense that a firm would expect a more-detailed presentation.

If the interviewer allows you to reuse the slides provided to you as background for the case, it's quite easy to create a long and detailed presentation very quickly.

Regardless of presentation length, the structure is always identical. Whether it's a one-slide presentation or a 30-slide presentation, the high-level structure is the same:

Conclusion

- Supporting point 1
- Supporting point 2
- Supporting point 3

Restate conclusion

The difference between short and long presentations is the level of detail. You might use the classic synthesis structure exactly as above on a single slide, while in a 14-slide presentation you might use the same structure and add another level underneath each supporting point:

Conclusion

Supporting point 1
- Supporting chart 1A
- Supporting chart 1B
- Supporting chart 1C

Supporting point 2
- Supporting chart 2A
- Supporting chart 2B
- Supporting chart 2C

Supporting point 3
- Supporting chart 3A
- Supporting chart 3B
- Supporting chart 3C

Restate conclusion

In this expanded structure, the fundamental argument is the same, but three charts are referenced that bolster each supporting point.

Two Example Structures

A five-slide presentation that uses the "collapsed" structure might look like this:

- Slide 1 — Conclusion: Client should sell off XYZ division.
- Slide 2 — Supporting point 1: The division has never been profitable.
- Slide 3 — Supporting point 2: Competitors have an insurmountable cost advantage.
- Slide 4 — Supporting point 3: Given industry pricing, competitors can sustain current pricing profitability, but we will perpetually lose money.

- Slide 5—Restate conclusion: Given these factors, we recommend selling off XYZ division.

Using the "expanded" structure, we might have a 14-slide presentation that looks like this:

- Slide 1—Conclusion: We should shut down or sell off the XYZ division.

- Slide 2—Supporting point 1: The division has never been profitable.

- Slide 3—Subpoint 1A: It has had at least a 10 percent negative profit margin in each of the past ten years.

- Slide 4—Subpoint 1B: It operates in a commodity market with average pricing across competitors varying less than 0.5 percent.

- Slide 5—Subpoint 1C: Because prices can't be changed and variable manufacturing costs are 10 percent higher than unit prices are, it's impossible to be profitable without lowering variable costs.

- Slide 6—Supporting point 2: Unfortunately, competitors have an insurmountable cost advantage.

- Slide 7—Subpoint 2A: Each of our top five competitors has ten times our market share.

- Slide 8—Subpoint 2B: This results in the top five competitors having a 10 percent variable cost advantage over us.

- Slide 9—Subpoint 2C: In addition, we lack the $1 billion in capital needed to increase production by ten times.

- Slide 10—Supporting point 3: Given industry pricing, competitors can operate profitably indefinitely while we lose money.

- Slide 11—Subpoint 3A: It's impossible for us to raise prices to improve margin because prices have historically linearly tracked the variable costs of the most efficient competitor.

- Slide 12 — Subpoint 3B: Due to capital constraints, the cost position can't be improved.

- Slide 13 — Subpoint 3C: Because we can't win in this market, our only option is to exit this business by shutting down or selling to a competitor.

- Slide 14 — Restate conclusion: Given these factors, we recommend shutting down or selling off the XYZ division.

Each of the text points above would be the title of each slide. The body of each slide ideally would be some chart, data table, or visual exhibit that supports the slide's title.

If you wanted to expand the 14-slide structure even further, you could create three supporting sub-subslides under each of the nine supporting subpoints, and then your presentation would consist of 41 slides.

If you're math-oriented, you'll notice that this structure within a structure is analogous to a fractal. If you're not familiar with that concept, here's a simple demonstration: Stand in front of a big mirror and then take another mirror and point its reflective surface at the big mirror. If you look carefully, you'll see a reflection of a reflection of a reflection. Just as a fractal (or the mirror demonstration) is really a picture within a picture within a picture, synthesis is really a nested structural hierarchy consisting of a structure within a structure within a structure.

I'm not a mathematician or a scientist, so perhaps my analogy isn't completely mathematically accurate, but I hope it illustrates the concept effectively.

Creating a Good Slide

A good slide has three components:

- A chart or data table
- A chart label
- A title (the key message at the top)

Most beginning presenters create slides the wrong way — by copying presentations they've seen others make, not realizing that most everyone does it wrong. The most common mistake people make is to use the chart label as the title.

Let's walk through creating a slide, beginning with the chart or data table. We'll use the following data table showing the ten-year profit history of the client:

Year 1 — $1.0 million loss (-14 percent net margin)

Year 2 — $1.5 million loss (-19 percent net margin)

Year 3 — $2.0 million loss (-20 percent net margin)

Year 4 — $2.1 million loss (-21 percent net margin)

Year 5 — $1.8 million loss (-19 percent net margin)

Year 6 — $1.7 million loss (-16 percent net margin)

Year 7 — $1.9 million loss (-18 percent net margin)

Year 8 — $2.0 million loss (-20 percent net margin)

Year 9 — $2.1 million loss (-12 percent net margin)

Year 10 — $1.9 million loss (-18 percent net margin)

The next part of the slide we'll work on is the chart label. A good *label* explains what the data table shows and the time frame it covers: "XYZ Division — Historical Profits & Profit Margin Percentage (Year 1–Year 10)." Most presenters use an abbreviated version of the chart label to create the *title*: "Historical Profits for XYZ Division." The problem with this is that a label is typically a fact, not a conclusion or interpretation.

Consider the following questions when writing the title for each slide:

- What's the most important thing about the chart?

- So what?

What would you say is the most important thing about the chart above that we need someone to notice? I think it's that the division has *never* been profitable despite *ten years* of trying!

Another way to arrive at the same result is to ask yourself something that virtually every new McKinsey consultant is trained to ask (typically by repeatedly being on the receiving end of the question): "So what?"

Let's say a new consultant presents the above table to a

partner, saying, "Here's a ten-year historical trend of the client's profits."

The partner says, "So what? Why should I care?"

The new consultant, feeling a little embarrassed, says, "Because the client has never been profitable despite ten years of trying, so it might actually be impossible for the client to be profitable."

The partner says, "Ah, OK. I see. Now *that's* worth discussing with the CEO." And *that's* what the slide's title should be.

The first part of the consultant's response to "So what?" is a conclusion the chart supports factually: The client has never been profitable despite ten years of trying. The second part of the response ("so it might actually be impossible for the client to be profitable") is now in play.

A partner would typically say here, "Your point about the business never being profitable is an interesting hypothesis. How could we prove it?" If you've paid close attention, you know that an issue tree should come next, followed by analysis and then synthesis.

This hypothetical dialogue between consultant and partner is the same type of dialogue you want to have with *yourself* as you prepare a presentation.

Telling the Story

Did you notice that if you read *only* the titles from the 14-slide presentation in sequential order and never even see the exhibits, a story emerges? Let's see how the story reads if we read each slide's title, one right after another ...

We should shut down or sell off XYZ division.

The division has never been profitable. It has had at least a 10 percent negative profit margin in each of the past ten years. It operates in a commodity market with average pricing across competitors varying less than 0.5 percent. Because prices can't be changed and variable manufacturing costs are 10 percent higher than unit prices are, it's impossible to be profitable without lowering variable costs.

Unfortunately, competitors have an insurmountable cost advantage. Each of our top five competitors has ten times our market share. This results in the top five competitors having a 10 percent variable cost advantage over us. In addition, we lack the $1 billion in capital needed to increase production by ten times.

Given industry pricing, our competitors can operate profitably indefinitely while we lose money. It's impossible for us to raise prices to improve margin because prices have historically linearly tracked the variable costs of the most efficient competitor. Due to capital constraints, the cost position can't be improved. Because we can't win in this market, our only option is to exit this business by shutting down the business or selling it to a competitor.

Given these factors, we recommend shutting down or selling off the XYZ division.

Notice how the story works even if you present only the titles of each slide (and omit the actual exhibits). That's a mark of a good message.

And this story serves another purpose: It's the memo you present to the client. Memos aren't used in the interview process, but they have the same structure as—you guessed it—the slide presentation.

Practical Tips for Creating a Presentation

In some interviews, you will be expected to create a presentation from scratch—meaning you need to create the exhibit, the label, and the headline for each slide. For other cases, you may be permitted to reuse the slides (the charts and their labels) the interviewer gave you as background information (this is the preferred option) and handwrite the "so what?"-oriented slide title.

It takes some time to create your own slides, so manage your time carefully and create a concise presentation; otherwise you'll risk not finishing your entire presentation. It's better to have a 100 percent complete presentation at the 50 percent detail level than it is to have a 50 percent complete presentation at the 100 percent detail level.

If the interviewer lets you recycle exhibits, with some practice you can assemble a presentation—even a long one—fairly quickly by figuring out the storyline that forms the backbone of your argument. Once you've established the storyline, you find slides to support it. Here's the mechanical process for using provided exhibits to assemble a presentation:

1. Synthesize the case as you would in a traditional case interview and write on a piece of paper your conclusion and three supporting points.

2. Sort your slides into four piles: one for each of the three supporting points and one for points that don't seem to fit your structure.

3. Focus on one pile of slides at a time. Pull out the three slides from each pile that best reinforce and validate your supporting point. (Note: You don't need precisely three charts per supporting point. It's OK to have a few more or a few less. If you end up with more, determine whether you can consolidate your supporting points into a smaller, more concise set of points.)

4. Figure out the title for each chart, using the "so what?" self-questioning technique. Write or type the title at the top of the slide.

5. Organize each group of slides into the sequence that makes the most sense or is easiest to follow. You will present the slides in this order.

6. Repeat steps 3 through 5 for the remaining supporting points.

Presenting the Story

Don't simply read your slides during your presentation. When you open your presentation, state your conclusion up front and *then* explain the structure you will use to prove it.

In a conversational tone, state the key takeaway from each

slide. A great way to determine the takeaway for a slide is to fill in the blank in this sentence: "The key takeaway on this slide is _____." Then just repeat the filled-in-the-blank portion of the last sentence aloud for your audience. Once you've stated the "so what?" title of the slide, *then* explain the exhibit being shown to support the point.

Your verbal presentation shouldn't be a word-for-word recitation of your slides. Your audience isn't dumb; the interviewer can read faster than you can speak. It's a colossal waste of time and incredibly irritating to have a presenter read to you as if you're 4 years old.

The Communication Rhythm

The rhythm of the communication during your presentation will go something like this:

1. Direct attention to the appropriate slide.
2. Answer "so what?"
3. Explain the chart that proves the point.
4. Repeat these steps for the next slide.

If you are presenting via a computer, the rhythm is as easy as clicking the button to advance to the next slide (thereby automatically directing attention to that slide), stating your key takeaway message, and explaining the chart that proves the point. You'll also want to highlight any key anomalies the audience should notice.

If you are presenting via a photocopied presentation distributed to every member of your audience, prompt the audience to turn to the designated slide when you so indicate: "Now let's turn to slide 2." Once everyone's on the correct page, state your message and explain how the chart supports it. In practice, the communication rhythm sounds like this:

OK, let's turn to slide 2. You'll notice here that XYZ division has never been profitable in the entire history of the division. In ten years of attempts, nothing has succeeded.

(The message is similar to our earlier example but more conversational.)

If you look at the table on slide 2, you'll see a ten-year history of profits in both dollars and profit margin percentages. In the "best" year, we still had 12 percent negative margins. This business isn't now and never has been profitable, and as you'll see on slide 3, it's unlikely ever to be profitable, for two key reasons.

(Notice the segue in the last part of the sentence.)

First, this is a commodity business, so there's virtually no variation in pricing across competitors. As you see in this chart, a snapshot of pricing over the past five years, there's less than 0.5 percent variation in pricing. This is a nearly perfect definition of a commodity business.

On slide 4, you'll see the second reason why it's unlikely that this business will ever be profitable: economies of scale and cost structure. As you see on this chart, the top five competitors are all ten times our size in revenues. This gives them enormous economies of scale that, as you'll see on slide 5, translate into a 10 percent lower variable cost advantage. It's this advantage that's the critical difference between being profitable and unprofitable in this business. Every key player that's ten times larger than we are is profitable. Everyone else simply doesn't have the scale to be cost-competitive. Clearly, under the current pricing and cost structure, we're unable to make this business profitable.

On slide 6, you'll see that the amount of capital needed to get ten times larger exceeds what's available to us. We estimate it would take $1 billion in capital to achieve the economies of scale needed to compete with our top five competitors, based on their current cost structure, which further assumes they don't merge or invest in any additional capital infrastructure of their own. As you see on this chart comparing capital required and capital available, we're short by 80 percent. In other words, we just don't have the money to get bigger and more efficient.

As you see on slide 7, the data leads us to the inevitable conclusion that we cannot win in this market. Because we can't win, we have to question why we are even in this market. You'll see on slide 8 that our strong recommendation is to exit this market by shutting down the division to reallocate resources elsewhere or, if possible, by selling it to another player in the market.

Note how deliberately *conversational* the communication in the example is. By using language such as "In other words, we just don't have the money to get bigger and more efficient," the candidate drives the point home. Such language has a particularly strong impact when said aloud, because it's simple and to the point. Oftentimes it's easier to make such casual yet profound points verbally than to write them in the more formal tone expected in a written presentation.

PART SEVEN

Getting the Offer

Chapter 24

HOW TO GET MULTIPLE JOB OFFERS

CANDIDATES NEW TO the case interview process often think of the case interview as an exam of some sort, similar to one they might have taken in school. This common misperception overlooks a truly fundamental difference between an exam and the case interview. In most exams, you're tested on your knowledge of the material at hand. In the case interview, you're tested on your *habits* in *applying* what you've learned in a high-stress environment. There's a big difference between the two.

For example, it's one thing to answer a bunch of questions on an exam about how to ride a bicycle. To prepare for this exam, you might memorize the rules of the road, gear-shifting ratios, the proper sequence in which to apply brakes, and other key pieces of knowledge. To prepare for a bicycle race, on the other hand, you'd practice completely different skills, because ultimately you're measured on your final time in the race. A case interview is like a bicycle race: You're evaluated not on what you *know* but rather on what you can *do* when it counts.

Candidates who get multiple offers possess *both* case interview *knowledge* and highly disciplined case interview *habits* in applying that knowledge.

Why Consulting Firms Have Multiple Rounds of Interviews

Unlike many industries in which you might have one or two interviews before you get a job offer, in consulting it's not uncommon to have up to ten interviews throughout multiple rounds of interviews. Given the surprising consistency of this interviewing approach across different firms within the consulting industry, getting a job offer clearly doesn't happen by accident.

Why so many rounds?

Because the consulting firms are evaluating how *consistently* you apply what you know in solving cases. Luck may help you get one case right, but it's unlikely to help you pass eight very different cases in a row.

This book tells you what you need to know to pass the case interview, but to maximize your chances of success, you need to do more—just as you need to do more than read a book on how to ride a bicycle to maximize your chances of winning a cycling competition.

Winning a test of skills hinges on one key element: practice. In the context of the case interview, *practice* means honing your problem structuring, computational analysis, and logical reasoning skills; comparing your performance to that of proven role models; and seeking the guidance of a coach or mentor to point out errors you don't even realize you're making. By layering practical preparation on top of the wealth of information this book provides, you will maximize your chances of getting multiple offers.

When I look back on my own success in securing multiple consulting job offers (six from major firms before I started declining final-round interviews), I realize that my performance on any one case was pretty good, but my *consistency* is what led to multiple offers.

Many candidates passed one or two cases and then secured a job offer, but few candidates could do extremely well every single time, regardless of the firm's reputation, the interview format, or the particulars of the case. Having excelled in roughly 60 out of 61 case interviews, I can say unequivocally that my consistent performance stemmed primarily from extensive practice to develop highly *disciplined habits*.

Knowledge vs. Habitual Application

The gap that separates those who get offers from those who don't is the same gap that separates those who possess case interview theoretical knowledge from those who have made a habit of applying that knowledge consistently and effectively across all types of situations.

It's important that you recognize and appreciate this distinction, because it is one of the quirks of the case interview process that surprises candidates who discover the industry just a few days before their first interview.

The Benchmark: 100 Hours of Practice

By virtue of having one of the more prominent blogs (www.caseinterview.com) in the case interview preparation community, I often receive field reports from new consultants who have secured job offers by using my materials. Frequently, I'll ask them what they did to prepare for the case interviews and how long it took.

I've noticed a distinct trend among those who have received job offers: Of the candidates who received offers at the top three firms, 90 percent invested 50 to 100 hours in case interview preparation; approximately 10 percent invested around 10 hours.

The conceptual takeaway here is that by investing 50 to 100 hours in case preparation, you improve your odds of success tenfold. (Although the statistical validity of this assertion is imprecise, the point is that more practice leads to better performance.)

Another trend I've noticed among those who get offers is that many people didn't prepare sufficiently for their first interview with a top firm. Only after they were rejected did they understand just how high the performance bar in the consulting industry is. After such rejection, candidates realize they have a small number of interviews remaining, so they work extremely hard to prepare after the shock of the first rejection. There's no need to wait to be rejected before taking preparation seriously. What follows are the four steps to take on your way to case interview mastery and multiple job offers.

The Four Steps to Mastery

The path to mastering case interview skills and developing disciplined habits involves four key steps. Some candidates can skip a step or two and still get an offer, but to maximize your chances of success, follow all four steps:

1. Build knowledge
2. Find role models
3. Practice in a live setting
4. Seek assessment from a mentor or coach

Step #1: Build Knowledge

Building knowledge involves developing an understanding of the concepts, processes, and expectations surrounding the case interview. By reading this book carefully, you will have accomplished this step and have a solid understanding of how the case interview process works, what's expected of you, what you're supposed to do in a case interview, and why you're supposed to do it.

Step #2: Find Role Models

In Step #2, you begin to develop an experiential grasp of how the knowledge you learned in Step #1 translates in the real world. In other words, in this step you experience what a great case interview looks and sounds like.

You'll notice subtleties of the case interview only when you witness firsthand how a successful case interview unfolds. These nuances include how often you say certain things, how to maintain a relative balance between making assertions and asking questions, how to backtrack your analytical problem solving when you know you've overlooked something, how to know when to dive deep or troubleshoot more, and how to know when you've done enough to move on.

One of the best ways to learn these subtleties is to find a role model to emulate. You want your role model to role-play the part of the candidate. That way, when it's your turn to be the candidate, you'll have a clear mental and experiential picture of what you're supposed to be doing in the interview. By emulating your role model's performance, you can improve your own skills and performance incrementally, thereby getting closer to the level of your role model's performance.

If you have a friend or a friend of a friend who works in a top-tier consulting firm, ask to conduct a mock case interview with him or her as the candidate. Pay attention to specific nuances, including precisely how that person phrases certain statements, when he or she requests specific numerical data as opposed to general information, and how he or she handles a dead end.

If you don't have someone who can be your case interview role model, use resources like my Look Over My Shoulder (LOMS) program, which consists of more than 20 recordings of live case interviews with actual candidates—some did exceptionally well and eventually got offers from the top three firms, and others performed very poorly.

The LOMS program lets you eavesdrop on the best and worst of these interviews and hear commentary on the precise differences between these two levels of performance. It also provides aspiring consultants insight on the microscopically specific details of a case interview, such as deciding which adjectives to use in the interview and when, and why such precise communication is so important.

For more information on the LOMS program, visit www.caseinterview.com/jump/loms.

Step #3: Practice in a Live Setting

Once you understand what you're supposed to do in a case interview (Step #1) and have experienced a case interview firsthand by working with a role model (Step #2), the next step is to practice the case interview in a live setting with another person.

Simulate the case interview by sitting across from another human being who is looking you in the eye, asking you tough questions, asking you to do math, and asking you to develop insightful solutions to a vague business problem. The whole process can be pretty stressful!

Your case interview skills improve by leaps and bounds when you force yourself to practice with others. This is especially true once you internalize what you learned with your role model and compare it to your own practice performance.

If you don't have a role model or choose the wrong role model, live practice won't help much, because you'll likely tend to repeat and reinforce bad habits that you may not even be aware of.

In contrast, a strong role model will help you realize your bad habits, so during live practice you'll be hyperaware of and hypersensitive about your own performance. By comparing your own performance to your role model's, you'll gradually improve your case interview skills.

Ideally, your live-practice partner will be going through the consulting recruiting process too (this is common on college and business school campuses), or you can recruit a friend or family member to conduct practice interviews (spouses in business-oriented fields are common practice partners among married candidates).

The people I know who have secured offers from the top three firms participated in an average of 50 practice cases in preparation for their interviews. That's a lot of practice.

Regardless of your innate level of talent, I can guarantee that your performance on your 50th case will be dramatically better than your performance on your first case. If you're competing against a candidate who has had 50 live-practice cases and is doing her first case interview with an employer (making it her 51st case) and you're doing your first case ever with a real interviewer, your competitor has an enormous advantage.

If you don't have a qualified case interview practice partner, use www.CaseInterviewPartner.com, an online service that helps you find other aspiring management consultants to work with as case interview practice partners.

Step #4: Seek Assessment from a Mentor or Coach

Friends, family members, and peers can help you get a lot of practice interviews under your belt. This type of practice helps you become accustomed to the case interview process and eliminates the glaring mistakes most candidates make when they are new to the process.

Once you've had sufficient live practice, hold a few practice sessions with a highly qualified mentor or coach who is a current or former consultant at a top consulting firm. This person will have the depth of experience to notice the subtle mistakes you're making that a peer-level practice partner would not. Quite often these subtle mistakes separate the candidates who get offers in the final round from those who don't.

The differences in performance that lead to an offer from a firm instead of rejection in the final round are often quite small but, to the experienced interviewer, very noticeable.

Once you know what remaining bad habits you have that an experienced interviewer would immediately notice and count against you, you can focus your remaining peer-level training on correcting these bad habits and thus make the most of the limited practice time you have.

If you don't have access to consultants who are working or have worked for the caliber of firm you're targeting, engage the services of a case interview coach. I have several coaches on staff who provide this kind of objective assessment to many of my readers and students. These coaches are former McKinsey, Bain, and BCG consultants who are well-skilled in providing you with useful, actionable, and objective feedback.

For more information on case interview coaching, visit www.caseinterview.com/jump/coaching.

Chapter 25

HOW TO PROJECT CONFIDENCE

AS YOU MIGHT expect, consulting firms look for candidates who demonstrate confidence during the case interview. Before I explain how to project the confidence firms desire, I want to explain why consulting firms value confidence so much more than most people realize. To do this, it's useful to step back for a moment to view the business of consulting from a psychological perspective.

On the surface, it seems like a client outsources to a consulting firm the analytical work needed to make a big decision. Upon deeper inspection, we see that the client (the individual executive, not the corporation) is highly uncertain about an upcoming business decision. In many cases, the decision is a "bet your career"-type decision with extremely high stakes for the client's personal career.

The client's psychological motivation for hiring the consulting firm is to reduce the anxiety associated with a lack of clarity about the decision. In other words, the client isn't buying just analysis; she is buying *confidence* and *reassurance* about a particular course of action. If an individual consultant demonstrates a lack of confidence during a meeting or presentation—even if the hesitancy stems from, say, the consultant's inexperience with presentations rather than a lack of conviction in his recommendations—the client may end up feeling she's not getting what she wants (and subconsciously needs).

That's the main reason interviewers, especially those in firms where new consultants have client contact, assess a candidate's confidence level—to ensure that clients won't doubt the consulting team's conclusions. Because it's not uncommon for a client to pay $100,000 to $300,000 a month to hire a consulting firm, you never want the client to think to herself, *Why the hell am I paying that kind of money to listen to a consultant who is just as uncertain about this decision as I am?*

Ultimately, *consulting is the transference of confidence (in a decision) from the consultant to the client*, and it's hard for the transfer to occur if the consultants themselves don't appear confident in general or in the specific decisions they're recommending.

Confidence and the Extrovert

Many people perceive confidence as an inborn personality trait typically associated with extroverts. When I think of confidence, I think of either the natural-born salesperson or certain friends of mine who are very social and whom everybody knows.

In the context of the case interview, though, I don't think this general perception applies—or at least not as much as you might think. And here's why: The case interview isn't a social function. It's a demanding interview that requires acute critical-thinking skills.

The majority of my colleagues at McKinsey were introverts, according to the Myers-Briggs Type Indicator. Their confidence wasn't necessarily an innate trait but rather one born from having exceptional technical competence in the consulting profession.

Conversely, in just a matter of minutes in a case interview, you can shatter the confidence of a candidate who has a naturally confident personality but is weak technically. I know because I have done this personally—not out of spite but to test a candidate's competence. By asking just one or two reasonable questions, it is very easy for an interviewer to separate those with confident personalities from those whose confidence comes from extreme competence.

In short, it's incredibly hard to "BS" or fool a seasoned case interviewer merely by being a smooth talker who doesn't have the logic and analysis to back up what he says.

The Three Sources of Confidence

Outwardly projected confidence in case interviews comes from three places:

1. Extreme technical competence

2. Correct mental perceptions

3. Extensive practice

The absence of any one of these three factors dramatically increases the likelihood that you'll come across as nervous at some point in the interview.

Let's examine each source of confidence.

Confidence Source #1:
Extreme Technical Competence

One of the most useful courses I ever took at Stanford was on public speaking. Because virtually all the students in the class were new to public speaking, the topic of nervousness came up quite a bit. I'll never forget advice I received from my teaching assistant: "The No. 1 rule to being confident as a public speaker is to *know your material!*" This rule is particularly applicable to case interviews, which are a form of high-pressure public speaking.

If you want to appear confident in a case interview, you need to develop exceptionally strong case interview skills, because it's not enough to be only somewhat familiar with what is expected — you need to completely master those skills. In some types of interviews, you can project confidence through your personality; but in the case interview, the confidence can come only from technical competence.

To be perfectly candid, if you think that reading this book will fully prepare you for case interviews, you are sorely mistaken. This book is merely a starting point and should by no means be considered the end of your technical preparation.

And here's why: competition.

Interviewing and then getting offers from the very top firms is an extremely competitive process. For example, based on acceptance rate, it's at least 10 times *easier* to gain admission to Harvard than it is to McKinsey.

Here's another example: When I applied to McKinsey as a Stanford undergrad, 400 Stanford students had applied, and only 6 received offers. That's a 1.5 percent acceptance rate among just *Stanford students*, who themselves were part of the 7 or 8 percent of applicants to get into Stanford.

Many people are eager to work for the top firms, but far fewer are willing to do the work necessary to develop extreme technical competence in the case interview. Devote yourself to being very good at cases and you'll automatically find your confidence building as part of the process.

Confidence Source #2:
Correct Mental Perceptions

The second key to demonstrating confidence is to care—but not too much—about how well you do in the case. Caring too much will cause you to stress unnecessarily about the supposed importance of this one interview in relation to your future life or career. Ultimately, you want to guard against three mis-perceptions:

- Misperception of what's at stake
- Misperception of your relative capability
- Misperception of the interview as a one-way assessment versus a two-way mutual assessment of fit

Misperception of What's at Stake

People tend to get extremely nervous when they feel they *must* do well.

In American sports in particular, you hear about athletes "choking" under pressure. One example would be an extremely talented athlete who is participating in the last Olympics of his career. He's won medals before but never gold, and in his events he chokes and doesn't get the gold. He's nervous because he cares too much about the outcome at an emotional level.

Similarly, a candidate might think, "If I don't pass this interview, my career is over before it's even begun."

One of my ongoing fascinations is the psychology of performance. According to my research, an optimal amount of stress inspires us to perform well. If we care too little, we don't try hard enough and aren't alert enough to perform at our best.

If we care too much, the burden is overwhelming. If we care a lot but not too much, we channel that slightly nervous energy into great performance.

I remember giving a friend from school a practice case, and he had convinced himself that his previous 15 years of schooling and a lifetime of hard work would be meaningless unless he passed his next interview. His stress level had gotten so high that, in the middle of the practice interview, I asked him, "What is 2 + 2?"

He couldn't answer. His self-imposed stress was that overwhelming.

If stress is an issue for you, try writing 50 reasons why not passing a particular interview isn't a big deal (e.g., I have an interview with another firm next week, I can try again next year, I can apply to boutique firms instead of the top firms). This exercise should help you realize that even though getting rejected isn't fun, it's certainly nowhere close to the end of the world.

If your natural inclination is to care way too much, I recommend taking an even more aggressive approach: Find 50 reasons *not* to care about the outcome of any of your interviews. This will likely counterbalance your tendency to care too much, so that ideally you'll end up caring just the right amount.

This isn't always an easy exercise, but it's really important that you get to a place mentally where you don't care too much about the outcome.

Misperception of Your Relative Capability

Another source of nervousness is misjudging your performance and credentials in relation to those of other candidates or of new consultants featured in recruiting brochures and on websites.

This always made me nervous, and it probably still does—I routinely underestimate my own abilities and overestimate everyone else's.

But here's a secret: The people featured in recruiting brochures and on websites are the firm's *most* impressive people, not necessarily the average people within the firm. So if you're comparing yourself against the one person at XYZ firm who has an MBA from Harvard, an MD from Stanford, and a JD from Yale ... and who won an Olympic gold medal ... well, let me be the first to tell you: They aren't all like that!

In fact, only one or two people out of several thousand at a firm are that absurdly impressive. Be careful not to misinterpret the data points you see and extrapolate incorrectly to the rest of the population. In psychology, they call this tendency *availability bias*: Based on the part of the sample that's available for you to see, you assume the rest of the sample is identical. And quite often this just isn't true.

Misperception of the Interview as a One-Way Assessment vs. a Two-Way Mutual Assessment of Fit

The final common misperception is that the firm is the only entity doing an evaluation during an interview. The healthier perception is that the interview benefits both the firm and you.

How does it benefit you? Well, you get to determine whether you like the consulting profession and the people you meet at a particular firm.

Viewing the interview as a mutual assessment prevents you from coming across as desperate (i.e., not confident!). If you indicate that you really want to work at that firm, but they haven't yet decided whether they want you, the firm holds power over you. You need to counterbalance this.

So here's a trick: Even if you desperately want to work for a firm, convince yourself that it's a two-way evaluation. Not only are they deciding on you, but you're deciding on them too!

Confidence Source #3:
Extensive Practice

Conveying confidence in a case interview requires extensive practice to prove extreme technical competence under the pressure of a live interview.

Based on the hundreds of success story emails and thank-you notes I receive from my blog readers (www.caseinterview.com), I would estimate that 90 percent of those who have received offers spent 50 to 100 hours preparing and practicing for the case interview.

One of my blog readers was a Harvard Law student near the top of his class who spent 300 hours preparing and practicing for the case interview. All three of the top firms — plus myriad others — offered him jobs. He was not only incredibly bright but also an intense hard worker. Among the top firms, the majority of candidates are both smart and extremely hardworking — don't forget this.

On the opposite end of the academic credentials spectrum, another one of my blog readers was a student from a top 100 school who was in perhaps the top 35 percent of his class. He bombed every interview he had initially, so he decided to start taking this practice stuff seriously. He put in 100 hours of practice and landed an offer at a top seven firm.

When I applied as a candidate, I too ended up putting in 100 hours or so of preparation and practice. Once I joined McKinsey, I assumed everyone working there would be smart — and most everyone was. What I didn't expect was how hard everyone worked. When you're hired as a consultant at McKinsey, you likely won't be smarter than your colleagues (you hope to be as smart as they are, at best), and you likely can't work harder than they do (again, you work as much as they do, at best).

I share all this not to discourage you from applying but rather to give you a realistic sense of what it takes to succeed during your case interviews and your future career as a consultant. Hard work is an enormous component in both developing confidence and securing multiple job offers.

Chapter 26

THE TEN MOST COMMON
MISTAKES TO AVOID

NOW THAT I'VE covered the full range of concepts, skills, and knowledge necessary to succeed in the case interview, I want to recap in a single place the ten most common mistakes candidates make.

I have referenced these mistakes elsewhere throughout this book, so use the following as a checklist in evaluating your own performance in practice sessions. In post-interview debriefing sessions, most of the people I spoke with who made these mistakes understood intellectually that they were supposed to avoid them, but they made them anyway.

Quite often, insufficient practice is the primary reason candidates make these mistakes, even though they know they should avoid them. Simultaneously eliminating all the mistakes from your case interview practice is extremely difficult, so focus on correcting one bad habit at a time. Once you've fixed that one, work on another.

I know from experience that many people will scan the following list, conclude that it all sounds familiar, and assume their work is done.

But understand this: *90 percent of all case interview rejections are based on at least one of the ten mistakes listed below.* So if you're not passing your case interviews, consider the possibility that, although you might intellectually understand the mistakes and how to avoid them, perhaps you haven't practiced enough to internalize the good habits and eliminate the bad ones.

The following list is in chronological order of when during the interview the mistake is made:

1. No hypothesis
2. Framework or issue tree not linked to hypothesis

3. Framework or issue tree not mutually exclusive enough
4. Framework or issue tree missing a key factor
5. Key insight missed due to insufficient quantification
6. Key insight missed due to lack of qualitative questioning
7. Math mistake
8. Jumping around versus linearly, logically drilling down
9. Pursuit of analysis that's unnecessary to test hypothesis
10. Activity-based summary versus big-picture synthesis

Mistake #1: No Hypothesis

Many case interview beginners start a case by stating a framework and then ask the standard list of questions they're "supposed" to ask, based on the framework.

But where's the hypothesis? The case interview is all about applying the scientific method to solving business problems. Just like scientists always define a hypothesis before they conduct a scientific experiment, you always need to define a hypothesis before you conduct a logical "experiment" (i.e., analysis).

Once you have stated a hypothesis, every question you ask, every piece of data you request, and every framework (or portion of a framework) you use should directly and concretely lead you to proving or disproving that hypothesis.

If you're inclined to ask a question or pursue an idea that does not directly lead to proving or disproving the hypothesis, you must seriously question whether you should bother pursuing it. If a question or idea isn't absolutely, positively necessary to test the hypothesis, strongly consider ignoring it.

Mistake #2: Framework or Issue Tree Not Linked to Hypothesis

Most candidates know they're supposed to have a hypothesis and a framework or issue tree, and they know it's critical that the framework or issue tree logically test the hypothesis. But some candidates fail to connect the dots. They mechanically go through the case process: Got a hypothesis? Check. Got a framework? Check. But then they fail to think critically about whether they need to adapt the standard framework or issue tree to a particular case and hypothesis.

Here's a simple example: If your hypothesis is "Enough of the client's customers are insensitive to price increases, so raising prices would actually improve profits," then you don't need to use the section of the business situation framework that addresses the competition. It's not absolutely, positively necessary or critical to testing the hypothesis.

In contrast, segmenting the customer base and assessing the price sensitivity of each segment would be critical. These two questions, and perhaps one or two more (but not all), from the section of the business situation framework relating to customers would be relevant and absolutely, positively necessary to test the hypothesis.

This mini-example demonstrates what I mean when I say you need to learn to use the frameworks flexibly. Use only the bits and pieces that are most relevant in testing the hypothesis, and ignore the rest.

Mistake #3: Framework or Issue Tree Not Mutually Exclusive Enough

Sometimes a candidate will set up an issue tree that isn't mutually exclusive enough, so that it fails the ME portion of the MECE (mutually exclusive, collectively exhaustive) test. When a candidate says, "I want to look at these three factors to test my hypothesis," but the three factors overlap a lot, it's very confusing to the interviewer (not to mention clients).

Interviewers will often say in these instances that the candidate's problem-solving structure wasn't "simple" or "clean," or that it was "messy," "confusing," or "inefficient."

The categories of your issue tree don't have to be 100 percent mutually exclusive, but it's helpful and expected that they be mostly mutually exclusive.

For example, in the business situation framework, the four categories of analysis are customers, competitors, company, and product. Of these four areas, three—customers, competitors, and company—are fairly mutually exclusive. In general, customers tend not to be competitors, because competitors are separate from the client's company. Each of these three areas refers to a distinct and separate entity.

Products, however, aren't an entity. Products are a different concept entirely and aren't 100 percent mutually exclusive from customers, competitors, and company because products cut across all three areas.

In practice, the business situation framework is implicitly organized as follows:

- Customers (excluding product-related information)
- Competitors (excluding product-related information)
- Company (excluding product-related information)
- Product

This implicit organization is mutually exclusive enough for interviewers.

The most common cause of not being mutually exclusive enough is when candidates start thinking about *topics* instead of *categories* of topics. Another common cause is when candidates include topics from different hierarchies in the same level.

For example, let's assume your hypothesis is that in certain customer segments your client's products are seen as highly differentiated. Your issue tree structure might look like this:

Hypothesis: Client's products are differentiated in some (but not all) segments

- Customers' needs by segment
- Competitors' product offerings by segment
- Client's product offerings by segment

In this structure, you compare what customers want to what's available to them—looking at one segment at a time. While the above structure is mutually exclusive enough, take a look at how confusing the structure below is:

Hypothesis: Client's products are differentiated in some (but not all) segments

- Client's product X

- Competitors' products
- Client's products (all products)
- Customers' needs

In this example, the client's product X appears in two places: in the branch titled "Client's product X" and again in "Client's products" (because when we talk about all the client's products, we logically include product X) and is thus redundant. An alternate way to organize this would be as follows:

Hypothesis: Client's products are differentiated in some (but not all) segments

- Client's product X features
- Competitors' products
- Client's *other* products
- Customers' needs

By adding the word "other" to "Client's products," you improve the structure by making it mutually exclusive, but there's an even better way to organize this structure: Move "Client's product X features" and "Client's other products" so they're "nested" beneath a point titled "Client's products":

Hypothesis: Client's products are differentiated in some (but not all) segments

- Competitors' products
- Client's products
  - o Client's product X
  - o Client's other products
- Customers' needs

This structure is mutually exclusive and keeps the hierarchy level of the issue tree consistent and clean.

To avoid problems with the MECE test, take five to ten seconds to ask yourself the following questions when you're designing your issue tree:

- Does my structure list topics or categories of topics?

- In any given level of my issue tree, am I mixing categories, topics, and subtopics? (Hint: Categories, topics, and subtopics should all appear at the same level of the issue tree hierarchy.)

- Can I rephrase any categories to improve mutual exclusivity?

Mistake #4: Framework or Issue Tree Missing a Key Factor

Another common mistake candidates make is failing to include a key factor in their framework or issue tree. Recall that with the MECE test, you organize information (such as your issue tree or framework) in a way that's both mutually exclusive and collectively exhaustive. Sometimes the candidate's framework or issue tree is neither mutually exclusive nor collectively exhaustive, but failing to pass the CE portion of the MECE test is a bigger problem. When you're not mutually exclusive, your thinking is logical but a bit untidy. In comparison, when you fail to be collectively exhaustive, often your logical reasoning is flawed by the omission of something critical.

Assume, for example, the client in your case is trying to determine if it makes sense to enter a particular new market and, specifically, if the market is big enough. You can address the first part of that question by using portions of the business situation framework, but that framework won't work for the second part in determining if the market is "big enough."

The business situation framework is useful in identifying key issues, trends, and qualitative information, but it's weak in computational analysis. So you might need to take the customer and competitor analysis subcomponents of the business situation framework and expand them to address the more quantitative aspects of this particular case.

If your subhypothesis is that the market *is* big enough, the two factors you would use to test that subhypothesis would need to define quantitatively how big is big enough (typically, some criteria the client has on desired minimum level, market share, or revenues), and you'd need to estimate the market size and the portion of it the client might be able to get.

In other words, to answer the client's question and test the hypothesis, you'd need to take (on the fly) the "standard" business situation framework (especially the customer and competitor sections) and augment it with an estimation-type question in order to obtain sufficient information to test your hypothesis and answer the client's question.

In this example, just using the standard business situation framework would be insufficient to answer the *specific* question the client has asked. You must constantly be asking yourself if your structure is missing anything necessary to answer the question at hand.

Mistake #5: Key Insight Missed Due to Insufficient Quantification

Many candidates with liberal arts backgrounds tend not to use mathematical quantification often enough. As a result, interviewers perceive them as lacking precision or being inefficient in their problem-solving process.

For example, in a profitability case in which profits are down, sales are down, and costs are up, it's clear that the decline in profits is caused by both sales decreases and cost increases.

Many candidates will incorrectly assume that they need to analyze both causes. Instead of making this assumption, they should mathematically calculate what percentage of the profit decline is attributable to each cause and then focus the analysis on the area that contributed more.

Candidates should ask, "How much have sales declined by?" and "How much have costs increased?" and then decide where to focus. Candidates need to use quantitative data for every branch and sub-branch of the issue tree to justify where they want to focus and why it is the most factually justified place to focus next.

Mistake #6: Key Insight Missed Due to Lack of Qualitative Questioning

Candidates with math or engineering backgrounds commonly assume the entire case is one big math problem. In these instances, they do all the obvious math in the case and then realize they have no idea what's going on with the client. In addition, they can't isolate the underlying cause of the client's problems (symptoms, actually) and as such are unable to propose a solution.

The underlying issue here is the failure to gather qualitative data. In addition to asking how much a certain metric is, candidates need to ask questions such as the following:

- Why does the client price this way?
- The client emphasizes speed of delivery, so what do competitors emphasize? The same thing or something different? If different, what is it?
- How does customer segment A differ from customer segment B in terms of what they are looking for in suppliers?

You'll notice that all the questions above must be answered with descriptive language, not numbers. In most cases, you need to develop some *qualitative* understanding of the business in order to figure out what's going on with the client. Once you know what's going on qualitatively, *then* you use math to measure, quantify, and numerically compare the impact of various qualitative decisions the client made previously.

So if customer segment A cares about price and customer segment B cares about speed of delivery, you want to ask, "What percentage of the customer base comes from customer segment A versus customer segment B?"

The key to doing well on the case interview is bouncing back and forth between asking qualitative questions to build a conceptual understanding of the situation and then verifying that understanding numerically.

Mistake #7: Math Mistake

If you say during a case interview that 2 + 2 = 6, the interview is essentially over. Clients don't pay $100,000 to $300,000 a month for math mistakes.

Doing math quickly and accurately is ideal, but doing it slowly and accurately still gives you a chance at an offer. Doing math incorrectly, whether quickly or slowly, results in an automatic rejection 95 percent of the time, especially with a top three firm.

If you're interviewing with a top 20 firm and you make a minor math mistake (e.g., you misunderstood something as opposed to made a computational error), you might, if you're super-lucky, pass the interview if everything else was stellar.

In short, get the math right. End of story.

Mistake #8: Jumping Around vs. Linearly, Logically Drilling Down

Ideally, you should open your case with your hypothesis and list the three or four key factors you need to test your hypothesis. You want to follow this format:

My hypothesis is _____. The three key factors I'll use to test this hypothesis are:

- Factor 1: _____
- Factor 2: _____
- Factor 3: _____

You would then address each of these factors in the order listed (assuming you listed them in priority order, which you should have).

Because candidates who are creatively gifted often have a hard time thinking in this highly linear way, they are usually the ones who tend to make the mistake of jumping around based on what pops into their head.

For example, a candidate might start off with factor 1 and then say, "Oh hey, you know ... we should look at factor 4 too." At this point, the interviewer thinks, "Okay, where did that come from?" In the middle of factor 4, the candidate branches off laterally into factor 5 and seemingly forgets about factors 2 and 3. The candidate finds factor 5 so interesting that he may neglect to ask himself if an understanding of factor 5 is even necessary to test the hypothesis. Or if he realizes it's actually not that important, he may try to jump back to factor 3 and, if he doesn't run out of time, factor 2.

In contrast, the linear thinker says, "I'm going to cover factors 1, 2, and 3" and then promptly does so in that order (unless new information is uncovered that prompts a revision of the hypothesis and perhaps a revision of the three most important items on the list).

In consulting, the linear thinker is highly valued. The creative thinker, who often sees nonobvious, nonlinear connections between very disparate ideas, is not valued very highly.

Steve Jobs, for example, was an exceptionally creative thinker. He saw relationships in the world of technology, media, and creative design that few others noticed. Despite this enormous creative gift, he would have made a lousy consultant and quite likely wouldn't have been able to pass a case interview.

So clearly, creatively jumping around isn't a bad thing in life or in business, but it is in a case interview.

Mistake #9: Pursuit of Analysis That's Unnecessary to Test Hypothesis

Sometimes a candidate can solve cases and still get rejected. To the uninformed candidate, this can be incredibly frustrating.

An interviewer's feedback on the candidate's performance might be, "Yes, you got the right answer, but your approach was *inefficient.*" Consultants hate inefficient analysis for two reasons: It results in lost profits for the firm and jeopardizes the firm's ability to answer the client's key question within the financial budget allocated for the project. In other words, inefficient analysis is expensive.

Inefficient analysis stems from analyzing unnecessary things; it's asking for *more* than the minimum necessary data to test the hypothesis and running *more* than the minimum necessary computations needed to test the hypothesis.

This mistake typically happens for one of two reasons:

- Focusing on irrelevant issues
- Failing to run a "ballpark" analysis before running a detailed analysis

An issue is relevant to analyze if the answer you receive from the analysis would alter or reverse your potential conclusion. For example, let's say your client is looking to invest in a new factory and requires at least a 25 percent return on investment before it is willing to take the plunge.

After analyzing the biggest costs, which compose 85 percent of total costs, you determine that the return on investment is only 10 percent. You don't need to analyze the remaining costs, because even if you could somehow reduce the remaining costs to $0, there's no mathematical way to exceed the 25 percent return-on-investment objective.

The key to avoiding unnecessary analysis is to ask yourself constantly, "Does this specific analysis have the potential to conclusively disprove my hypothesis?" If an analysis has no chance of disproving your hypothesis, consider it irrelevant and skip it.

Mistake #10: Activity-Based Summary vs. Big-Picture Synthesis

Many case interview beginners close a case by listing everything they've discovered in the order they've discovered it. This chronological summary accurately describes what the candidate analyzed and discovered, but the interviewer (and the client) doesn't really care. She just wants to know up front what's important.

For example, in a merger and acquisition case, don't just list everything you did and the data you discovered, like this:

- First, I analyzed the sales growth of the target company and found that it's based largely on a single product.
- Second, I analyzed what's driving market growth and

found that the growth is likely to taper off in a few years.

- Finally, I looked at profit margins. While margins would improve due to cost savings from raw materials acquired under our procurement agreements, this improvement in margins is likely to be offset by anticipated declines in prices.

Instead, kick off the closing with a simple, concrete, and clear action-oriented decision: "Do not buy this company. It's a bad idea."

It's crystal clear, isn't it?

Of course, the interviewer will ask, "Okay, *why* is this a bad idea?" This is when you'll want to transition to sharing details, but only after you've established the big picture first.

By keeping an eye out for these ten most common mistakes during your practice efforts, you'll maximize your chances of passing your case interviews. In the next chapter, we'll cover some advanced case interview practice resources you should know about.

Chapter 27

ADVANCED CASE INTERVIEW RESOURCES

AS YOU TRANSITION from learning about case interviews to practicing them to participating in live interviews, you might find the following resources helpful.

Resource #1: Free Book Updates, Handouts, and Video Demos

Book updates and companion items are available for free on my website. In addition to updates, these bonus items include printable versions of the diagrams in this book and videos that demonstrate the techniques I've referred to.

To download these free companion items, visit www.caseinterview.com/bonus.

Resource #2: Math Practice Tool

This free math practice tool measures your math speed and accuracy. It focuses on computational math (as opposed to brainteaser-type math), which is used in both quantitative assessment tests and hypothetical situation case interviews. Access the tool at www.CaseInterviewMath.com.

Resource #3: Success Story Field Reports

I ask readers of my books, blog, and email newsletter to tell me about their job offers. These field reports describe the experience each person went through, what was easy or hard, what was surprising (or not), and the approach the candidate used to prepare.

You can find an archive of success story field reports by clicking on "Success Stories" at www.caseinterview.com.

Resource #4: Look Over My Shoulder Program— Recordings of Actual Case Interviews

The Look Over My Shoulder (LOMS) program contains audio recordings of case interviews with more than 20 candidates. The recordings include my voice-over commentary on what a candidate is doing well or poorly as he or she is doing it.

This book is a "learn by reading"–type resource, and the LOMS program is a "learn by emulating/doing"–type resource. I highly recommend the LOMS program as the next step in your case interview preparation. You can learn more about the program by visiting www.caseinterview.com/loms.

Resource #5: Find a Case Interview Practice Partner

Once you've started emulating a case interview role model, you'll want to practice case interviews with a partner. If you don't have friends, family members, or classmates with appropriate case interview skills with whom to practice, consider using the case partner matching system I developed. It matches you with other candidates who are actively looking for practice partners, and it can match by time zone, language preference, and type of case practice desired.

Find more information about this service by visiting www.CaseInterviewPartner.com.

Resource #6: Work One-on-One with a Case Interview Coach

If your time for live practice is limited and you want to achieve the greatest results in the shortest amount of time, it may make sense to work one-on-one with a case interview coach. Even if you have time to practice cases with a partner, it's useful to get an objective external evaluation of your case interview skills to determine your current level of proficiency.

Due to popular demand, I have several case interview coaches on staff to coach my readers and students. All of them are former consultants at the top consulting firms: McKinsey, Bain, and BCG.

For more information on this service, you'll want to visit www.CaseInterviewCoach.com.

Closing Thoughts

I can't emphasize enough the importance of practice. It sounds trite, but practice really does make perfect—especially in a highly competitive field such as management consulting.

When two equally talented candidates face their first real case interview, the one who invested 50 to 100 hours in preparation has an overwhelming competitive edge over the one who spent just an hour or two.

Getting multiple job offers in management consulting comprises three activities: Follow the proven process I've outlined in this book, use the practice resources around you (or the ones I've suggested), and work really hard. That's the secret.

I wish you both good practice and good luck in your recruiting process.

***

I love hearing about the success of my readers. To tell me about your job offers and other successes, send an email to joboffers@cascinterview.com.

Also let me know what you think of this book by sending an email to bookfeedback@caseinterview.com. Although I'm not always able to reply, I do read all my emails.

Lightning Source UK Ltd.
Milton Keynes UK
UKOW051854170613

212391UK00002B/512/P